JANE AUSTEN STEPPING WESTWARD

An Introduction to Jane Austen and her
Experiences in the

West of England

Compile[

Penelope To[

"What, you are stepping westward?"

The dewy ground was dark and cold;

Behind, all gloomy to behold;

And stepping westward seemed to be

A kind of 'heavenly' destiny:

I liked the greeting; 'twas a sound

Of something without place or bound;

And seemed to give me spiritual right

To travel through that region bright.

William Wordsworth, 1807

White Fan Talks Publishing

White Fan Talks Publishing

First Published 2015

whitefantalkspublishing@gmail.com

ISBN 978-0-9932849-0-8

9 780993 284908 >

A CIP catalogue record for this book is available from The British Library

Compiled by Penelope Townsend

Design and Layout by Wotton Printers

Printed in Great Britain

by

Wotton Printers, Newton Abbot, Devon

Set in Palatino Linotype

Dedication

For Richard Crispin Townsend 1944-2012

Thanks to Sam & Isabel, Fen, Rob, Meredith & Percy, Ellie, Jo & also Effy

Cover Picture: Dawlish, Devon early nineteenth century

INTRODUCTION

This book is meant to entertain you. It is a tribute and celebration of all the amazing times I've enjoyed in Devon, sharing a love of life and literature with many wonderful people. I am proud to be among the millions of readers who find the stories of Jane Austen quick moving, funny, light hearted, shrewd and honest. Their wisdom helps at every turn in the road. As works of genius they are not only unsurpassed in their construction, but they can still be experienced with as much enjoyment as when she first read them aloud to her family. I have tried to draw a picture of Jane Austen's family background and her life in her twenties. During these years she came to visit the West Country and lived in Bath. The experience inspired her and the influence of the travels she made from Bath can be perceived throughout her work.

I do not claim to be an author but would quote Montaigne: *I have gathered a posie of other men's flowers and nothing but the thread that binds them is my own.*

There are the occasional fictionalised accounts of events. Although based on received wisdom, they are just personal frolics.

You will find all my acknowledgements at the end of this small work. Every care has been taken to acknowledge sources and seek permissions.

I have included many quotations from her books and letters so that you can hear her witty voice for yourself. I do so hope you enjoy hearing of her West Country experiences. We might like to watch the films her work has inspired, read the prequels and spinoffs but

Dear Friends – Please, please Read *Jane Austen!*

Reading Jane Austen, Northernhay, Exeter

6

Contents

Chapter One - Jane Austen's Family

Pretty joy!

Sweet joy but two days old,

Sweet joy I call thee;

Thou dost smile.

I sing the while

Sweet joy befall thee.

William Blake 1757-1827

A Winter Birthday – A Warm Family

Jane Austen's mother, Cassandra, had her birthday on 29th September 1739. So when she found herself expecting her seventh baby in 1775 she realised she would be thirty six before it was born in November. I wonder whether she attached any importance to the fact that she was *'more nimble and active than I was last time'*. It might have occurred to her that the way she was carrying the baby meant it could be a little girl. She had five boys already. This could be a sister for Cassy who *'talks all day long, and in my opinion is a very entertaining companion'* A second girl would fit in well in such a male dominated household with five sons. At some time in the 1770s the household also included several schoolboys who boarded with the family and were tutored by Rev. Austen.

But Jane was in no hurry to join the melee it seemed, and took her time to arrive. She was to be a Saturday's child who according to the old rhyme *works hard for its living*. She did not put in an appearance until 16th December 1775. It was so cold a winter that Rev. Austen baptised her at home the next day and didn't take her to Steventon Church until 5th April. He wrote to spread the good news *we were in old age grown such bad reckoners but a month later than expected the time came, and without a great deal*

9

of warning, everything was soon happily over…she is to be Jenny

Jane Austen's early life was spent in Hampshire, as her father, George Austen was the Rector of Steventon and nearby Deane. The Rectory seems to have been a rambling old place. Today its remains sleep beneath pasture. The site was recently excavated and the finds are in Basingstoke Museum. It was demolished in the 1820's and a new Rectory built for Jane Austen's nephew, William Knight , by his father Edward. William was to be rector for many years. Perhaps by the time of its demolition the old house was in too poor a state of repair to do otherwise.

Jane had six brothers; James, the oldest, became a clergyman with literary aspirations. He took over the living from Rev. George Austen. The second son, George, appears to have suffered from fits, perhaps what we now know as epilepsy. He lived very privately with Mrs Austen's brother, who was also an invalid. They were not far away from Steventon at Monk Sherborne, cared for by the Culham family.

The third son, Edward, was adopted by the rich and childless Mr and Mrs Thomas Knight, second cousins to George Austen. He took their name and inherited estates in Kent and Hampshire.

Her brother Henry was outgoing and lively. He is sometimes reckoned Jane's favourite brother. Henry entertained her in his London homes and showed her a little of Society. He became a Soldier then went into Banking. When the Bank failed he took Holy Orders to be a Clergyman. He helped Jane Austen a great deal in her dealings with publishers. He certainly enjoyed the reflected glory of his association with such a talented sister.

The youngest two brothers, Francis and Charles, were both in the Royal Navy. Francis became an Admiral and Charles a Rear Admiral. George Austen was determined they should be properly prepared for their careers and sent them to the Navy's Royal Academy at Portsmouth at the age of twelve years old.

Charles was spoken of with particular affection by his sisters. He was noted for his kindness and good sense towards the men under his command and led by excellent example. Francis was open handed and kind hearted to his family. He ended his dificult career as a distinguished admiral.

Both had very long careers at sea. It was a hard life of duty with promotion uncertain. Francis was proud to be 'one of Nelson's captains' and asked that this should be his memorial epitaph. At 91 he was the last surviving sibling of Jane Austen. He is buried at St Peter and Paul, Wymering, Hampshire. Charles died in service, aged 72, and was buried at Esplanade Burial Ground Trincomalee, Skri Lanka.

Jane and Cassandra

Jane appears to have loved her sister Cassandra with an almost anxious devotion and admiration.

They were united through their shared childhood and later, whenever temporarily apart, they kept in touch with a stream of affectionate and newsy letters.

Cassandra had a childhood friend, Thomas Fowle, who came as a pupil of George Austen. They became engaged to be married, but he died abroad, of Yellow Fever.

At the time of his death he was ordained and waiting for an ecclesiastical living, which would mean he could afford to support a wife. In the meantime he was accompanying a relation, Lord Craven, on an expedition to the West Indies. 'Making your way' in any sphere often depended upon the favour of a mentor who could help your career to prosper. The engagement was secret and certainly Lord Craven expressed regret that he had asked Tom to go with him, which he would not have done had he known of this commitment. In the event neither of the sisters married. Maybe they were *wedded to each other* as their mother described them. They were both staunch in the belief that one should not compromise and should only marry for the deepest affection.

When Jane died, Cassandra was bereft: *'a treasure, such a Sister, such a friend as has never been surpassed-she was the sun of my life, the gilder of every pleasure, the soother of every sorrow'*

A Little Bit of Mischief

An outwardly demure girl has been allowed to sit quietly in her father's study while he works on polishing his sermon. It is very quiet on this late September day. She is glad of the crackle of the fire which warms her cold hands because she is practising her writing and everyone knows how hard that is with stiff fingers.

She can hear the distant hum of conversation as her mother, Mrs Austen, directs cook in the preparation of dinner. It reminds her that she is so very hungry and her concentration wanders.

On the table sits the Parish Register. The pages at the beginning show specimen entries. Clergymen might see how to record the banns. If you wanted to marry someone, you had to tell the people where you lived and whom you wished to marry. They might have an objection and must have a chance to say so. The banns, which were a notice to marry, were read three Sundays running in Church. Most people went to Church unless they were ill, so this gave everyone a chance to know who you intended to marry. It was quite a family occasion to go and hear your banns read. Good practise for bashful grooms to gain courage. In those days when it was regarded as essential to marry, brides to be might try not to look too much like the cat that got the cream. Jane Austen wrote to her niece, Fanny Knight:

Single women have a dreadful propensity for being poor-which is one very strong argument in favour of matrimony

<u>*(Letter 13th March 1817)*</u>

The Register also had a sample page to show how to record the marriage itself.

All of a sudden, a mischievous impulse makes temptation irresistible. Perhaps a little dreamy in the heat, Jane's imagination begins to roam. To whom would she like her name to be *joined in matrimony*?

A husband whose name linked him to heroes of British History would be *most* suitable. Jane liked history. So she chose four names:

Edmund, after first Patron Saint of England, then *Arthur*, after the heroic king and lastly *William* after the Conqueror. On the other hand a fine husband could bear the robust name of a plain man, *a Jack Smith*. So she chose that name too.

Her father was totally absorbed and did not notice as the Parish Register slid quietly across the table. He might have noticed that Jane was especially busy. He might have smiled a pleased smile. He liked her to be industrious. Jane carefully entered her 'marriage' to Edmund Arthur William Mortimer and also to Jack Smith. But why stop there? She was sure her writing was improving. Jane Austen wrote a pretend form for banns to be published between her and one Henry Frederic Howard Fitzwilliam.

Did she think there might be a punishment for this scribble? Certainly as an aunt she mentioned a *thump or two*, as a possible 'correction' for youthful misdemeanors. Maybe she thought it would be worth it, or did not think at all. Her wise and gentle father would be far more likely to see the humour. She had done no real harm. After all it was a writing exercise of a sort.

It was this quick bright, precocious mind which matured into genius. No childhood impressions were lost, just as Jane Austen's experiences and knowledge of Somerset, Dorset and Devon, even as far as Plymouth, were woven into her brilliant social comedies.

Jane Austen lived within a tightknit household of family members, servants and paying pupils. She followed faithfully in the shadow of her older sister. It was in her family circle that she shone and felt safe.

Links were maintained with extended family through letters and visits. Jane's mother had a sister, Jane who was married to a Doctor of Divinity, Edward Cooper. They had a son, Edward and a daughter Jane.

In 1783, when Jane Austen was seven years old, she went with Cassandra and this same cousin Jane to be under the care and tuition of widow Mrs. Cawley, Edward's sister. Mr and Mrs Austen set off on a short holiday journey, their first for some time. Unbeknown to them or Jane Cooper's parents, Mrs Cawley decided to relocate to Southampton. An alarm was raised when Jane Cooper managed to send her mother a message that she and the other two girls were all ill with typhus. The fever must have been brought ashore by sea farers. Jane Austen was seriously ill. Mrs Austen and Aunt Jane mounted a rescue expedition at once. The girls recovered, but sadly Aunt Jane Cooper died of typhus.

Jane had a happier experience of schooling in Reading later. Cassandra and Jane flourished under the care of the Matron, Sarah Hackitt. She was known as Madame , La Tournelle, which no doubt impressed prospective parents. They gained a little knowledge *scrambled themselves into a little education* as Jane later described it . Madame, La Tournelle must have been a constant source of wonder, with her strange cork leg and stories of actors and actresses. She loved the theatre. Altogether it must have left happy memories, for Jane Austen, replying to a letter which she has enjoyed reading, remarks: *I could die of laughter at it, as they used to say at school (Letter to Cassandra, 1ˢᵗ September, 1796)* Before her teens Jane Austen's formal education was at an end.

How would this young woman strike others? Fulmar William Fowle, a friend of her brothers, describes Jane Austen : *'She was pretty – certainly pretty. Bright without question, and a good deal of colour in her face – like a doll – no that would not give at all the idea, for she had so much expression – she was like a child, quite a child, very lively and full of humour – most amiable, most beloved.*

Jane Austen's high spirits and lively behaviour attracted some criticism in her youth, reportedly being described by Mrs Mitford as skittish:

'..The prettiest, silliest, most affected husband hunting butterfly she ever remembers''

Jane Austen was obviously ready to be introduced to the shocking and exciting phenomenon of eighteenth century society, a visit to Bath.

The Austen family knew the City of Bath well, as we shall now discover.

<u>Love in Bath –A Successful Alliance</u>

Proud City of Bath with your crescents and squares,

Your hoary old Abbey and playbills and chairs,

Your plentiful chapels where preachers would preach

(And a different doctrine expounded in each),

Your gallant Assemblies where squires took their daughters,

Your medicinal springs where their wives took the waters,

The comely young faces of buildings and wenches,

The cobbled back streets with their privies and stenches-

How varied and human did Bath then appear

As the roar of the Avon rolled up from the weir.

Extract -*The Newest Bath Guide by John Betjeman*

Jane Austen's mother was named Cassandra after her great aunt, the Duchess of Chandos. Tradition has it that the First Duke of Chandos encouraged the architect and builder John Wood the Elder to build beyond the old mediaeval city walls of Bath. These walls encircled the Abbey lands and the surrounding settlement. John Wood took the Duke's advice and the first venture was Queen Square (built 1729-36).

From here development of the City occupied all available land, embracing the hills and even the water meadows across the River Avon (by way of the new Pulteney Bridge). Great Pulteney Street and the airy regions of Lansdown became the sought after places to stay.

Queen Square was where Jane spent a very happy family stay in Bath in 1799. By the time she finished the first draft of *Persuasion in 1816,* her character, Louisa Musgrove. protests against staying at such an old fashioned location 'none *of your Queen Squares for us Papa'*

Bath's popularity was such that during the eighteenth century the population grew from 3,000 to 30,000.

A Wedding at Walcot Church, Bath 26th April, 1764

Jane Austen's own West Country Links began here with the story of her parents' marriage.

The Bridegroom

George Austen was a man who had learnt hard life lessons from his personal family history. He was orphaned at six years old and raised by his father's sister, Aunt Hooper, in Tonbridge. He surely took to heart the words written by his widowed Grandmother Elizabeth Weller. She left a Memorandum for herself and her heirs.

Elizabeth Weller believed that her children would succeed if she ensured they had a good education.

'I always tho't if they had Learning, they might ye better shift in ye world'

Through help which George Austen received from relatives, he gained not only an education, but also a great respect for the importance of family. Jane was proud of this much loved father. He was a fine scholar in Latin and Greek at Oxford University and appointed to supervise the behaviour of the undergraduates, known in this role as the *'handsome Proctor'*.

The Bride

The Master of Balliol College had a niece named Cassandra Leigh. She was living in Bath with her widowed mother. Cassandra and George Austen were well matched .Cassandra's sparkle and spirit were complementary to his more serious academic temperament. . Her family were known for producing persons of quick witted humour .The all too few surviving letters and accomplished verse written by Jane Austen's mother, whether describing her life, counselling schoolboys or celebrating her recovery from ill health, show that the future Mrs Austen certainly shared this trait and passed it to her daughter.

In appearance she also had large grey eyes and what we might call 'a nose of character', rather fine and distinctive. She was very proud of this, considering it a mark of her good breeding. No cosmetic surgery needed or wanted.

The marriage seems to have been successful. There was respect between the parties, affection and good humour. The usual trials were met in the usual way *'Mother's angry, father's gone out'* is a pithy comment written in Jane's copy of *Fables Choisies*, though not necessarily by her.

The new Mrs George Austen needed to be tough and determined. Although used to a rather less strenuous existence, she took to country life with enthusiasm and purpose. Mrs Austen also took care of the boys who came to be tutored by Mr Austen for university entrance. It appears possible that when she judged it necessary Mrs Austen took refuge in hypochondria to remind her family of the strain of raising a family as a dutiful eighteenth century wife. It is also likely that Cassandra Austen's state of health arose from the physical consequences of childbearing and hard work. Suffering from 'nerves' was a suitably genteel complaint for ladies of the gentry class. Jane Austen turned this to comedy in *Pride and Prejudice.*

Mrs Austen's relations, the Leighs, were a distinguished family. In particular there were the Leigh family at Adelstrop in Gloucestershire and the ennobled Leighs at Stoneleigh Abbey in Warwickshire. All were descended from the Elizabethan Thomas Leigh, Lord Mayor of London. Mrs Austen was very assiduous in keeping in touch with 'the Cousinage' as she called the extended family.

The couple were married in St Swithin's Church in Walcot, Bath on 26th April, 1764. George was thirty three, Cassandra twenty four years old. The new Mrs. Austen wore a fashionable red wool travelling dress in the style of a riding habit. She had an overnight stay at Andover by way of honeymoon. The dress was the main item of her wardrobe for the next few years and ended its life cut up and up- cycled as a jacket for Francis to wear out hunting on his pony, Squirrel.

George Austen had been instituted Rector of Steventon in Hampshire thanks to his benefactor, a distant cousin, Thomas Knight of Kent. The living at nearby Deane followed in 1773, thanks to Uncle Francis Austen.

Another Bath connection was the Reverend Doctor Edward Cooper. He married Cassandra Austen's sister Jane and at one time they lived in Royal Crescent. They had a son, Edward and a daughter Jane as mentioned before. Dr Cooper moved away from The Crescent after his wife's death from typhus.

Chapter Two – Early Visits and a Terrible Trial

'Even before the Romans, we are told Celts and their animals wallowed gratefully in Bath's soothing ooze and ever since visitors have managed to combine Taking the Waters with Living it Up – Jan Morris, New York Times, 1982.

Two Visits to Bath – 1797 and 1799

1797

Who can ever be tired of Bath? (Northanger Abbey)

During November and December in 1797 Jane made her first recorded visit to Bath, during the popular winter season. Visitors would flock in for a stay of up to six weeks.

No letters survive from this stay, but perhaps the best tribute to Jane Austen's impressions of Bath is her novel *Northanger Abbey*.

Susan was the original working title of this work. It was drafted in the enthusiastic verve generated by Jane's first Bath experience. It was sold for £10, neglected, repurchased for the same amount, substantially revised and finally published in 1818 by Henry Austen.

Mrs Austen, Cassandra and Jane came to stay at Number One Paragon, Bath. It was the home, during half each year, for James Leigh Perrott, Mrs. Austen's brother and his rich and autocratic wife, Jane.

The entry into Bath was over the Old Bridge .It's modern day counterpart is The Churchill Bridge.

In *Persuasion* we have a glimpse of how Bath was experienced by Jane Austen on her first visit from the quiet of the countryside, filtered through Lady Russell's partiality:

'Everybody has their taste in noises as well as in other matters; and

sounds are quite innoxious or most distressing, by their sort rather than their quantity. When Lady Russell, ..was entering Bath on a wet afternoon and driving through the long course of streets..amidst the dash of other carriages, the heavy rumble of carts and drays, the bawling of newsmen, muffin-men, and milkmen, and the ceaseless clink of pattens, she made no complaint. No, these were noises which belonged to the winter pleasures; her spirits rose under their influence.'

Jane Austen was writing for her contemporaries, for those persons with experience of the gothic romances such as Ann Radcliffe's *Mysteries of Udolpho* .But she did not wish to add to the genre but find another voice of her own, of serious themes delivered with delicious humour. She wrote for people who were enjoying the melodramatic tales set in glamorous locations, but who could also laugh at their absurdities.

Bath was a perfect location because it was unique. The exotic stylishness lent itself to parody. Jane Austen was writing for experienced readers who would understand her jokes. So it is no surprise that the teenage heroine of *Northanger Abbey*, Catherine Morland, imagined the journey to Bath to be full of the type of difficulties and lucky accidents encountered by the heroines in the books she enjoys.

After all, in the *Mysteries of Udolpho* the coach is overturned and this accident leads to Emily St Aubert meeting her hero Valancourt. However Catherine's journey to Bath:

'..was performed with suitable quietness and uneventful safety. Neither robbers nor tempests befriended them nor one lucky overturn to introduce them to the hero'

Mrs. Allen thinks she has left her clogs at the inn, but then finds them. (Mrs. Allen, Catherine's kindly and ineffectual chaperone is in comic contradiction to Madame Montoni 's character in *'Udolpho')* . *Madame Montini* is a calculating character, cold and imperious. She behaves cruelly to the poor heroine.

Catherine's extensive knowledge of *horrid,* terrifying romantic novels has prepared her for the mischievous behaviour of lords and baronets if she should meet them. Her mother entertains no such suspicion. Mrs Morland confines herself to the type of advice familiar not only to Jane Austen's eighteenth century readership but to anyone parting from their mother for a while.

'I beg, Catherine, you will always wrap yourself up very warm about the throat when you come from the Rooms at night: and I wish you would try to keep some account of the money you spend; I will give you this little book on purpose'

In this story Jane Austen takes Catherine through all the delights and novelties for which Bath was famous. From Catherine's comfortable lodgings in Pulteney Street her adventures begin. She sets off to the Upper and Lower Assembly Rooms in the evenings and during the day visits the shops and admires all the parts of the town.

Catherine also travels by sedan chair, the useful mode of transport invented for the narrow Bath streets. After a happy evening with her new friend, Henry Tilney, Catherine goes home …

'Her spirits danced within her as she danced in her chair all the way home' (Northanger Abbey)

Introductions

Convention demanded that in order to socialize two people must be formally introduced. Mrs Allen and Catherine run up against this difficulty on their visit to The Upper Assembly Rooms. Abandoned by Mr Allen, who has deserted them to play cards all evening, the two ladies stay in social isolation amongst the crowded company. In fact Catherine can only glimpse the tops of the swaying feathers adorning the heads of the dancers.

On their second outing , Mr King, the Master of Ceremonies

at the Lower Rooms in Parade Gardens (which no longer stand), comes to their rescue. It is a rare example of Jane Austen including a real life character in her stories.

He introduces Mrs Allen and Catherine Morland to a young clergyman, Mr Henry Tilney. This entertaining fellow charms Mrs Allen with his sardonic appraisal of muslin gowns. He then quickly endears himself to Catherine by play acting as a foppish dandy . He takes her through the litany of Bath attractions:

'Have you honoured the Upper Rooms?

'Yes sir, I was there last Monday'

'Have you been to the theatre?'

'Yes, sir, I was at the play on Tuesday'

'To the concert?'

'Yes ,sir, on Wednesday'

'And are you altogether pleased with Bath?'

'Yes-I like it very well'

'Now I must give one smirk, and then we may be rational again'

Henry is obviously well acquainted with the routine of amusements.

He is also using the chance to get to know Catherine. Dancing provided a rare opportunity for private conversation in an age of closely chaperoned women. Before they part he remarks that she will have plenty to recall. She rejoins:

'Oh! Who can ever be tired of Bath?'

Henry's reply indicates that he is a fair way to being smitten!:

'Not those who bring such fresh feelings of every sort to it, as you do'

He admires her straightforward manner and warm heart. There is a suggestion that these are rare qualities in visitors to Bath.

Henry enjoys the amusements Bath has to offer for the six week stay, which most people found quite long enough. He doesn't make fun of Catherine's enthusiasm , but he does point out that there are more sensible uses of time away from its artificial atmosphere

Visitors to Bath gathered in The Pump Room to gossip, as they still do today. It overlooks the Baths. Fanny Burney was an author who Jane Austen admired. Fanny Burney was very fond of Bath. She has **her** naive character Evelina, in a book of the same name, express shock at the public bathing: *'At the pump-room I was amazed at the public exhibition of the ladies in the bath; it is true their heads were covered with bonnets, but the very idea of being seen, in such a situation, by whoever pleases to look, is indelicate'*

We certainly have no information that the experience of bathing in the Bath waters tempted Jane Austen in the slightest. But medical remedies were few at the time. Invalids were grateful of any ease in their symptoms. Drinking the water and bathing in it was a very popular cure for those who had indulged in rich living .

The Pump Room had just been renovated before Jane's first recorded visit to the City in 1796. Today it still has the Pump to supply glasses of the medicinal waters, the statue of Beau Nash and the clock made by Thomas Tompion.

A scene in *Northanger Abbey* is set near this very clock where Mrs. Allen renews her friendship with her school friend, now Mrs. Thorpe, and hears at some great length about all her children. She herself is childless.

'Mrs Allen was forced to sit and appear to listen to all these maternal effusions, consoling herself, however, with the discovery, which her keen eyes soon made, that the lace on Mrs. Thorpe's pelisse was not half so

handsome as that on her own'

Mrs Thorpe's eldest daughter, Isabella, soon proves herself a deliciously unsuitable companion for Catherine. They visit the Pump Room together. Isabella decides to consult the Book of Intelligence where there was a record of society arrivals and their addresses.

"'Do you know, there are two odious young men who have been staring at me this half hour. They really put me quite out of countenance. Let's go and look at the arrivals. They will hardly follow us there"

Away they walked to the book; and while Isabella examined the names, it was Catherine's employment to watch the proceedings of these alarming young men

"They are not coming this way, are they? I hope they are not so impertinent as to follow us. Pray let me know if they are coming. I am determined I will not look up."

In a few moments Catherine, with unaffected pleasure, assured her that she need not be longer uneasy, as the gentlemen had just left the Pump Room.

"And which way are they gone?" Said Isabella, turning hastily round. "One was a very good-looking young man"

Isabella sets off in hot pursuit, with Catherine keeping company.

On this occasion the young men cross what is now known as Abbey Churchyard and go under the archway to Cheap Street They cross over, while the traffic detains the young women.

Isabella is lacking in judgement, but as a girl without much of a personal fortune she is only trying to take advantage of what Bath had to offer; a chance to marry.

This was a preferred souvenir of your visit to Bath; a rich husband or a rich wife. It was an excellent place to be introduced to prospective spouses. Perhaps that is why Mr Elton rushes off to Bath after being refused by Emma in Jane's novel of that name. He is not disappointed. He marries Miss Augusta Hawkins. It is a whirlwind courtship, which seems somehow to be quite usual in Bath.

' ...he had not thrown himself away-he had gained a woman of £10,000. or thereabouts; and he had gained her with such delightful rapidity-the first hour of introduction had been so very soon followed by distinguished notice; the history which he had to give Mrs Cole of the rise and progress of the affair was so glorious-the steps so quick from the accidental rencontre, to the dinner at Mr Green's, and the party at Mr Brown's —smiles and blushes rising in importance-with consciousness and agitation richly scattered-the lady had been so easily impressed-so sweetly disposed-had in short , to use a most intelligible phrase, been so ready to have him, that vanity and prudence were equally contented'

This wooing had an outcome which suited both parties.

W.H. Auden amusingly refers to the commercial basis on which some eighteenth century marriages were arranged amongst the upper and middle classes. He rightly infers it was anything but 'polite society' in his poem *Letter to Lord Byron*. Auden professes himself shocked by *'the amorous effects of brass'*. Marriage could be a financial as much as a social and romantic transaction.

Bath was the happy hunting ground for rakes and fortune hunters. Some of the men in Jane Austen's novels, such as Willoughby, Captain Frederick Tilney, Henry Crawford, Wickham, Frank Churchill or William Eliot, who make visits to Bath are also **not** those most likely to safeguard any ladies' reputation. They would certainly be attracted by wealthy young women. Mr Allen makes immediate and careful enquiries about Mr Henry Tilney as soon as he notices him dancing with Catherine.

Mr Allen himself enjoys another most popular pastime, playing cards for money in the elegant octagonal card room at the Upper

Assembly Rooms. It has a minstrel's gallery for music to be played on Sundays, when card playing was forbidden.

Gambling was something of a mania during the eighteenth century.

The fashionable sport of horse racing provided an opportunity for gambling.

Bath had a permanent racecourse on Lansdown after the Blathwayt family of Dyrham Park gave permission in July 1811, though racing had started intermittently in 1728. In Jane Austen's novel *Mansfield Park* Tom Bertram is anxious to be at Bath to witness a race where he has a horse running. He and Henry Crawford obviously patronize the same livery stables. They are typical of a class of young men with money and similar tastes.

Jane Austen was far from prim and proper. With so many brothers and other boys at home there was no room to be 'coy or missish'. In her teens she invented short stories with lots of jokes about human weakness, including mentioning that it was advisable for a lady to have a strong head for liquor.

The impressions she gained during her visits to Bath appear in the form of all sorts of tiny details in her work which make it authentic.

Poor Invalids

Gout was one well known affliction which brought many visitors to Bath to get relief bathing in the warm waters and drinking large quantities of it, while eating a plain diet, including Dr Oliver's biscuits.

Dr William Oliver (1695-1764) worked hard with other influential persons such as Beau Nash to get people to subscribe to what has become the world famous Mineral Water Hospital.

A fee levied upon admission the hospital covered the cost

of transport home, or a decent burial if attempts to cure you were not successful. This was a service for the less wealthy. The affluent visitors to Bath could expect personal attention, prescriptions and large bills. Jane Austen was friendly with the daughters of Dr. Mapleton of Circus, Bath and her mother was attended by Dr Bowen. Dr Perry , a character in Jane Austen's work *Emma*, is always available to soothe the fears of the valetudinarian Mr Woodhouse as to his state of health. Dr Perry is saving up for a carriage, and his patients are helping him to pay for it.

Dr Oliver is buried in the graveyard at All Saints' Church, Weston, a village to the west of Bath and a favourite destination for Jane Austen when walking. Jane Austen never mentions the biscuits, but she does write about Dr Oliver's other invention, the Bath bun. She speaks of them with relish as being very good on a journey and also just the thing to top up Aunt Jane Leigh Perrot's meagre meals, even if they did 'disorder our stomachs'.

Dr Oliver abandoned Bath buns in favour of his biscuits in the end. We may still enjoy Bath buns with their currants and lump of sugar in the middle. But the patients of Dr Oliver were gaining rather than losing weight with such a treat. Upon his death he entrusted his recipe for Dr Oliver's biscuits, long known as Bath Olivers, to his coachman, Mr. Atkins, also giving him £100 and 10 sacks of fine wheat flour. Atkins opened a successful shop in Green Street, Bath and prospered. The Bath Oliver biscuits are still popular today.

Jane Austen's uncle, James Leigh Perrot, was a sufferer from gout. In *Northanger Abbey* the reason for Mr and Mrs Allen's visit to Bath was Mr Allen's gout. Jane's brother Edward feared he would also succumb, though happily this was not so. In *Persuasion* Admiral Croft was: *ordered to walk to keep off the gout, and Mrs Croft seemed to go shares with him in everything, and to walk for her life to do him good.*

Known since Egyptian times, Gout was later dubbed ' the arthritis of the rich 'by Hippocrates, whereas rheumatism was the 'arthritis of the poor'. Gout has been associated with a rich diet and too much fine wine right from the start. As such there was no stigma attached to it in places like 18th century Bath. It was more a badge of honour that showed you could afford the rich lifestyle which caused it. Gout was moreover thought to keep other diseases at bay. How strange.

In the 17th Century Thomas Sydenham, a foremost physician of the age described an attack as follows:

'The patient goes to bed and sleeps quietly until about two in the morning when he is awakened by a pain which usually seizes the big toe, but sometimes the heel, the calf, the leg or the ankle. The pain resembles that of a dislocated bone ..This is immediately succeeded by a chilliness shivering and a slight fever..

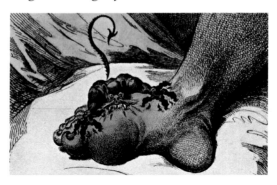

The pain...which is mild in the beginning, grows gradually more violent ever hour... so exquisitely painful as not to endure the weight of the bedclothes nor the shaking of the room from a person walking briskly therein'

Even stranger is the part Gout played in Britain's loss of the American Colonies. William Pitt the Elder suffered an attack of gout which kept him away from Parliament.

In his absence the Stamp Act was passed, which forced the colonists to pay a tax to cover the costs of defending the Colonies against the French, even though they were unwilling to pay. Pitt had it repealed on his return but later during another sick leave the heavy duty on colonial imports of tea was passed which led to the Boston Tea Party. [T.L.S. 1981, Pat Rogers]

One thing led to another and the Declaration of Independence followed in 1776. Adam Smith remarked famously in Book 4 of The Wealth of Nations:, published in that very same year:

"They will be one of the foremost nations of the world"

He wisely suggested that the colonies be represented in the British parliament. Like most far sighted ideas it was ignored. So America went her own way…

And all through a pain in the toe!!

All manner of remedies were tried besides the healing waters. Bath Herald advertised Whitehead's Essence of Mustard as a remedy for not only gout, but also complaints of the stomach, lumbago and palsy.

The widow Mrs Smith, a character in *Persuasion,* is a sufferer from rheumatic disease. This invention of this character shows that Jane Austen was acutely aware of the desperate circumstances of some poorer invalids in Bath. Anne Elliot seeks out her old school friend despite her father's disapproval.

Mrs Smith's accommodation is *'a noisy parlour and a dark bedroom behind'.* She has lost husband, money and health. But she has been fortunate in the help of her landlady's sister, Nurse Rooke. This *shrewd, intelligent, sensible woman* has helped Mrs Smith by keeping her in touch with the current gossip of Bath Society and nursing her. The creation of Nurse Rooke is a sort of alchemy. Perhaps Jane Austen got a germ of an idea from the existence of the Charitable Repository (1797) in nearby Bath Street .*This existed for the encouragement of industry in all descriptions of persons reduced to distress, by affording them a ready sale for their articles and paying them the full value when sold, without any deduction .*

(Bath Directory 1812, quoted by D LeFaye 3rd Ed. Jane Austen's Letters)

But in *Persuasion* the personal agency of Nurse Rooke links Mrs Smith to other parts of the story and Nurse Rooke's more affluent patients. The good lady encourages her patient to make small items for sale to the gentry, such as Mrs Fitzpatrick, housebound because she is expecting a baby. Her husband has been admired by the shallow Sir Walter Elliot solely on the grounds of outward good looks.

Bath -Full of Fashionables

Mrs Allen, guardian of teenager Catherine Morland   in Northanger Abbey states:

Bath is a charming place, sir: there are so many good shops here - we are sadly off in the country (She lives 9 miles from Salisbury)

Mrs Allen is very preoccupied with fashion. Jane Austen's letters reveal that those visiting Bath or London frequently shopped for relatives. She talks at some length of prices and patterns.

The Walcot Street area was known for bargains and Jane Austen seems to relish tracking them down. Her personal allowance was modest and even in those days did not give her a very great spending power.

In fact she is interested in fashion herself and enjoys shopping for others, though with some justification she admits she does not like buying them shoes! But in her books characters preoccupied with their appearance and in particular their clothes tend to be portrayed as shallow.

Great Pulteney Street, where Jane Austen places Mr and Mrs

Allen in comfortable lodgings with Catherine Morland is indeed convenient for the shops.

..here one can step out of doors, and get a thing in five minutes says Mrs Allen gleefully.

The shops on the Pulteney Bridge are famous, and it is only a short walk to the centre. After Catherine comes back from her walk round Beechen Cliff :

having occasion for some indispensable yard of ribbon, which must be bought without a moment's delay, walked out into the town and in Bond Street overtook the second Miss Thorpe, as she was loitering towards Edgar Buildings between two of the sweetest girls in the world, who had been her dear friends all the morning.

In *Persuasion* Sir Walter complains that he *once counted eighty seven women go by without there being a tolerable face amongst them'* as he stood in a shop in Bond Street, but it was a frosty morning, most unkind to fair complexions.

As Catherine walks past the shop at the end of Pulteney Bridge she might look up towards Camden Place. In Jane Austen's other novel to have a setting partly in Bath, *Persuasion* , the spendthrift Sir Walter Elliot hovers on the point of bankruptcy on the teetering edge of a precipitate and insecure location. Jane Austen's joke makes us aware that in every way he is 'on the edge'! Camden Place was planned as a crescent, but the end houses would not stand. As his lawyer, Mr Shepherd skilfully makes him realise that in Bath he can be *important at comparatively little expense.*

Milsom Street, where General Tilney is lodging and just above Bond Street, is one of the most fashionable locations to reside in Bath. It is here that Isabella sees *the prettiest hat you can imagine* in a shop window. It has coquelicot ribbons (poppy red). This was a very on trend colour at the time.

Jane Austen's imagination was fired by all the sights and sounds of Bath and its shops. Mollands pastry shop, famous for marzipan, became the setting for Anne Elliot's encounter with newly arrived Frederick Wentworth. His annoyance in seeing her whisked away by William Elliot pricks him to jealousy which forces him to examine his feelings and renew his courtship.

Further up Milsom Street on another occasion Anne meets up with Admiral Croft looking at the prints, usually satirical cartoons, in the print shop window. But in his bluff wisdom it is not the cynical joke that the artist may have intended which puzzles him:

Here I am, you see staring at a picture. I can never get by this shop without stopping. But what a thing here is, by way of a boat! Do look at it. Did you ever see the like? What queer fellows your fine painters must be, to think that anybody would venture their lives in such a shapeless old cockleshell as that? ...I would not venture over a horsepond in it.

The Sailor in him insists on things being straightforward and correct.

Royal Crescent-A Superior Location

Just a short way further up the hill beyond the Upper Rooms and the Circus is Royal Crescent.

The method of constructing a crescent of houses is to build the two end houses and sell them to raise the money to build the rest. John Wood was worried that it would not sell as it was not centrally situated in the city. After the stay of Frederic Augustus, Duke of York, the second son of George III , John Wood was justified in calling it the *Royal* Crescent – it worked like a charm and people thronged to live there.

Behind the façade with its 114 Ionic Roman columns and graceful semi-elliptical sweep each house has its own distinctive character.

The famous people and even fictional characters who have occupied houses in the Royal Crescent are many. In 1798, William Wilberforce courted Barbara Spooner, daughter of a rich business magnate from The North of England who was at Number 2. His name has become synonymous with the passage of legislation which finally led to the abolition of slavery.

Jane Austen's Uncle, Rev. Dr Cooper, a Doctor of Divinity lived at Number 12 1771-84.

The Linley family occupied number 11. The beautiful Elizabeth Linley, an accomplished singer, eloped from the house in a sedan chair to marry the playwright, Richard Brinsley Sheridan.

Even the fictional hero, known as The Scarlet Pimpernel was awarded Number 16 for his 'retirement' from rescuing distressed French aristocrats. His creator, Baroness d'Orczy obviously thinking this was a suitably fashionable setting for him.

The Vicomte du Barre set out from Number 8 to fight a duel with his former friend Captain Rice on Claverton Down in 1778. After holding extravagant card parties, trying to make a fortune from the gambling fever of the time, they had quarrelled over sharing £600 winnings. The Vicomte never returned. He lost the duel, but died lying across the boundary between two parishes on the top of Claverton, neither of which would bury him.

The charity of the Parish of Bathampton, a village on the outskirts of the City means he has a resting place in their churchyard.

Every house has its own story. Number 1 is now a museum and recreates the house as it might have appeared when it was the home of Henry Sandford between 1776 and 1796.

Jane speaks in *Northanger Abbey* of Mr and Mrs Allen bringing Catherine up here *'to breathe the fresh air of better company'*.

Beneath the Crescent the ha-ha is still visible. This is a ditch and wall to stop animals getting onto the lawns. It would not interfere with the view from the houses. In those days the fields ran straight down to the river and the Victoria Park did not exist.

1799

Jane's second recorded visit to Bath was to 13 Queen Square. This was from 17th May to late June 1799. The party included her brother Edward, who was wealthy due to his being adopted by a rich, distant cousin, his wife Elizabeth, their older children, Fanny and Edward, Mrs. Austen and Jane. Cassandra was not with them and this means there are wonderful detailed letters. When the devoted sisters were apart they wrote about three times a week.

It seems appropriate at this point to reassure those who might feel it is prying to experience such private correspondence. I should point out that Cassandra has relieved you of such nicety of conscience by obliterating any comments she thought might excite hurt or general unwholesome curiosity. She also burnt many letters.

Letters kept branches of the same family in touch They were shared between members of the households at either end. Think of it as a sort of Georgian intranet or link up.

It is a matter of conjecture as to why Jane Austen does not mention national events or politics or religion.

The preface to the first edition of the letters gives a wise clue. There is an emphasis on the importance of **domestic** details :

Four of the letters written from Queen Square were bundled up by Cassandra and given to her niece, Fanny. She would doubtless have had the intention of reviving happy childhood memories of a family holiday.

The whole tone of the letters is bright, irreverent and teasing.

The trip starts well with a veritable feast during the overnight stay at Devizes which included asparagus, lobster and cheesecakes.

Jane was well pleased with 13 Queen Square. It had large rooms and a good view of Beechen Cliff in one direction. Beechen Cliff was a favourite destination for some of her long walks round the City. The other way it was then possible to see Gravel Walk, mentioned in *Persuasion*. Jane had a bedroom on the same floor as Mrs Austen:

Nice sized rooms with dirty quilts and everything comfortable.

Jane reports that the house is looked after by a widow, Mrs. Bromley. She is delighted by the presence of a little black kitten scampering up and down the stairs.

Hetling Pump Room and Other Remedies

Edward was worried about his health. He took the waters at the Hetling Pump Room. (There were three pump rooms served by different springs at the time).He also bathed in the waters at The Hot Bath opposite, now part of the Bath Thermae Spa.

Part of your 'Bath cure' might include electric shock treatment. Jane Austen's comment about her brother Edward receiving it during this visit to Bath with him is that *I fancy we are all unanimous in expecting no advantage from it.* Experiments with electricity had scarcely reached more than the drawing room amusement stage. With a charge of static made by rubbing two separately charged substances together, several people standing in a row could all enjoy a little shock!

With the luxury items in which Bath abounded Edward could eat his way out of his crisis. The cheese which he went out to taste on his arrival was within easy walking distance over the famous pavements. He sent out for tea, coffee, sugar etc. to be delivered.

In *Persuasion*, Anne Elliot's younger sister,   Mary Musgrove complains that the terrible February weather makes it hard to get around. She is jealous of Anne having the smooth Bath pavements to walk upon.

Commissions

The letters are full of discussion and detail of items which Jane Austen has been asked to purchase. Current fashions are mentioned:

Flowers are very much worn & Fruit is still more the thing. Elizabeth has a bunch of strawberries and I have seen Grapes.........

I cannot help thinking that it is more natural to have flowers grow out of the head than fruit-What do you think on that subject?

After an exchange of letters cloaks for both Jane and Cassandra are made and ready to take home. A black lace a veil for sister in law Mary is added to the stock, after the first choice of black muslin is unsatisfactory.

Walking

Jane described herself as a desperate walker, and during this holiday she walked out to the village of Weston, and on another occasion : *We took a very charming walk from 6 to 8 up Beacon Hill, & across some fields to the Village of Charlcombe, which is sweetly situated in a little green valley, as a village with such a name ought to be.*

Sydney Gardens

At the beginning of June, 1799 Jane writes to Cassandra that she and Elizabeth are particularly excited to be going to a firework display for the King's Birthday. Jane is obviously not much of a fan of concert music. She cheerfully speculates that the size of the Sydney Gardens means that with any luck she can be at a distance where she won't be able to hear it!

In the event the Gala had to be postponed because the English summer then was no more predictable than it is now.

Jane later reports going to the repetition on the 18th June. They did not go along until after dark and loved the fireworks which were even better than she'd hoped

'We did not go till nine & then were in very good time for the Fire-works, which were really beautiful. & surpassing my expectation; - the illuminations too were very pretty

Although Jane Austen had no inkling of it in 1799, the existence of Sydney Gardens would be very important in her life when she became a Bath resident, as she lived at 4 Sydney Place, directly opposite the Gardens, for four years.

Cassandra and Jane Austen made full use of the circular walk around the park.

It covered about sixteen acres, with interest given to the walks by waterfalls, grottos and pavilions. There was a labyrinth and a bowling green. The King's Birthday Gala was only one of four or five regular events of the same sort during the summer.

There was also an amusement park element with Merlin Swings. These were like giant swing boats designed by a gentleman who was interested in the effect of gravity upon health.

The newly constructed Kennet and Avon Canal passed through the gardens, with its elegant wrought iron bridges.

A programme of public illuminations set up around the park could be enjoyed into the 1950s. One wonders what Jane Austen would have thought of the illuminated showpieces purchased from Blackpool Corporation and displayed in 1956. Her sharp eye would have seen their shabbiness. Those which were on a nursery rhyme theme might have subject matter well known to her. The writer certainly has an abiding memory of Little Miss Muffet, with a fearsome spider of giant proportions guaranteed to frighten anyone away.

Lady Noble, a resident of Royal Crescent in the 1950's took the trouble to write to The Times complaining of *'vulgarities and errors of taste'* which were *'as remote from Jane Austen's day as can well be imagined'*. Now what is it that Jane Austen says ? Ah yes:

'One half of the world cannot understand the pleasures of the other'

Jane Austen appreciated one aspect of the delights of Sydney Gardens which could be enjoyed in the public rooms at its entrance, as mentioned in her letter 2nd June 1799 . She flippantly says the family will avoid starvation by enjoying breakfast out at the Gardens.

'There was a very long list of Arrivals here, in the Newspaper yesterday, so that we need not immediately dread absolute Solitude - & there is a public breakfast in the Sydney Gardens every morning, so that we shall not be wholly starved'

The letters from Bath also have little messages dictated by Fanny and Edward enquiring after the chaffinches' nest in the garden. The children also report enjoying gooseberries in all forms- pies and puddings. They send their love to each member of the family and don't forget to send a message hoping: *all your turkies, ducks, chickens and guinea fowls are very well* . Fanny and Edward are getting the taste for letter writing and beg for another printed letter, to which they will reply.

The last letter before leaving Bath contains a discreet hint to Cassandra: *It is rather impertinent to suggest any household care to a Housekeeper, but I just venture to say that the coffee mill will be wanted every day while Edward is at Steventon as he always drinks coffee for Breakfast.*

The trial of Mrs Jane Leigh-Perrot

It is impossible to tell whether Jane Leigh Perrot suffered from kleptomania. What is certain is that she showed wonderful resilience in the face of a terrible situation and that she enjoyed complete support from her husband throughout her trial. The following account shows how muddled the situation was and how the rich could be vulnerable to extortion.

On the corner of Bath Street and Stall Street there was an haberdasher's shop called Smith's. Mr Smith had run away from his wife and financial problems and been declared bankrupt.

The shop was under the management of Mr Smith's sister-in-law, Elizabeth Gregory and her lover, Charles Filby.

The Trustees for Mr Smith's creditors were William Gye and Lacon Lamb. Gye had a printing business in Westgate Buildings. It is presumed that Gregory and Filby planned to blackmail Jane Leigh Perrot after she went into the shop on 7th August and enquired after lace. Wealthy woman like Jane Austen's aunt, Jane Leigh Perrot were sometimes the target of such unscrupulous and criminal attempt at blackmail by false accusations.

On 8th August 1799 she returned to Hot Bath Street, which was close to the Pump Room, while her husband James was taking the medicinal waters. She visited Smith's the haberdashers and bought a card of black lace to trim a cloak . She claimed to be unaware that an additional card of white lace was slipped into her parcel.

As Mr and Mrs Perrot walked past the shop later Gregory came out and asked if Mrs Leigh- Perrot had any white lace in her possession. The couple showed her the unopened parcel. Gregory opened it, removed the white lace and went back into the shop. Filby ran out and asked for their name and address, which was given.

Four nights later an anonymous note was received addressed to Mrs Leigh-Perrot, Lace Dealer. Gregory and Filby went to the Bath Magistrate and laid a charge of 'stealing lace to the value of twenty shillings' against Mrs Leigh-Perrot. This was grand larceny, a very serious offence. A potential capital punishment was usually commuted to transportation to Australia. On Wednesday 14th August Mrs Leigh-Perrot was committed to the Somerset County Gaol at Ilchester to await trial at Taunton Assizes the following March.

At Ilchester the Leigh-Perrots lodged with Governor Scadding and his wife. The accommodation was shared with the Governor's five young children and numerous pet cats and dogs.

It was suggested that Cassandra and Jane might go and keep them company. But to their credit Jane Leigh-Perrot refused, saying that she felt it was no place for young gentlewomen.

The Trial took place on Saturday 29th March, 1800. Gregory, Filby and the shop girl, Sarah Raines all gave evidence. The Counsel for Mrs Leigh-Perrot was able to discredit Filby, casting doubt on his honesty and good character.

Although the law at the time did not allow Mr Leigh-Perrot to speak for his wife, she was allowed to bring character witnesses to testify to her good character. The judges summing up took over an hour, and after fifteen minutes the jury returned a verdict of 'not guilty' Cheers and applause greeted the result. James Leigh-Perrot had already stated he would go to Australia with his wife if it came to that, so it must have been an enormous relief that she was acquitted.

The trial had taken its toll. Mrs Leigh-Perrot was described as appearing pale and emaciated after her ordeal. The trial itself had lasted seven hours. The cost in legal fees was two thousand pounds.

Chapter Three – 'The littleness of town life'

Jane Austen's Residency at Bath 1801-1806

(Bath) *suits us very well. We are always meeting some old friend or other; the streets are full of them every morning; sure to have plenty of chat; and then we get away from them all, and shut ourselves into our lodgings, and draw in our chairs.. Admiral Croft-Persuasion chapter 18*

This cosy picture of life in Bath for the Crofts is what George Austen and his wife, Cassandra Austen envisaged for themselves when they retired to Bath in 1801. It was an urban retirement after nearly 40 years in the country. They still had their two unmarried daughters at home, but the boys were all out in world. They were busy about their careers, but did not forget their sisters. It is in May 1801 that Charles presented Cassandra and Jane with the gold chains and topaz crosses they treasured all their lives.

Jane Austen's introduction to the West Country may have begun early in her adult life. But it was her residence in the City of Bath which brought her into the region which was to be so significant in her own life and a vital inspiration in her writing.

'A removal from one set of people to another… will often include a total change of conversation, opinion and idea' Persuasion chapter 6

There has been a long held belief that Jane Austen was very upset at news of the upheaval in her life caused by her parents' sudden decision to move. Family anecdotes have even suggested that she fainted when the proposal was sprung upon her. She had been staying with her dear friend, Martha Lloyd at Ibthorpe. The impression is that Mrs Austen was so excited that she scarcely gave her daughter a chance to get into the house before telling her.

Mary Austen, wife to Jane Austen's oldest brother, James was present at the time of the announcement. She reported Mrs Austen's words: '..*It is all settled, we have decided to leave Steventon in such a week and go to Bath'.*

But is seems likely that at the age of 25 she was resilient enough to resolve to make the best of the situation. In her novel *Persuasion* Jane Austen expresses a desirable response to adversity in Anne Elliot's admiration of her old school friend, Mrs Smith who exhibits *that elasticity of mind, that disposition to be comforted, that power of turning readily from evil to good, and from finding employment which carried her out of herself.*

There was no possibility of removing all the household possessions from Hampshire to Somerset. The Austen family took only their beds and personal possessions. James was to become Rector in his father's place and move to the Steventon Rectory. Jane Austen felt the surrender of so much very keenly. She saw the familiar objects of her early life go with many pangs. It must have been so hard to see everything moved from family pictures, her beloved piano, even to the brown mare taken away prematurely by James, who could not wait. But for a reader and writer, helping to sell Reverend Austen's library of over 500 volumes was especially painful. It was also galling that the 200 which were sold at public auction only fetched £70.

But out of this unsettled time Mr Austen had one proposal which raised Jane Austen's spirits and gave her something to anticipate with pleasure: *'summers by the sea or in Wales'.*

These excursions were very much part of his retirement plan. Mrs. Austen was not so keen, but was jollied along to join in the Devon and Dorset holidays which formed an important refreshment and relief during the following 4 years.

The prospect of the move may have been painful, but Jane Austen was a young woman, full of spirit and she was soon writing to her sister in a joking vein about 4 Sydney Place, the new home the Austen's had found after a slightly frustrating search.

They considered South Parade, but it was too hot

Where will you keep your bees? Jane writes to Cassandra. Alas, like pretty much everything else they are left behind in the country

King Street bedrooms are too small. Green Park seems unhealthily damp, although the Austen family lived there at a later date.

4 Sydney Place was chosen. It stands at the bottom of Great Pulteney Street. There would be no need to keep a carriage as Bath was small. Sydney Place was a level and short walk to the centre of the City.

The house was about 9 years old, part of an ambitious plan for building on the Bathwick Estate which was never completed. It was at the edge of the city and the rental was 150 pounds p.a. –George Austen had an annuity of £600 p.a. They would be comfortable, able to keep servants and afford to have seaside holiday.

Saturday 3rd to Monday 5th January 1801

Jane jokes that her mother is intending to hire two housemaids, an expense for which she has not prepared her husband

'My Mother looks forward with as much certainty as you can do, to our keeping two Maids – my father is the only one not in the secret. – We plan having a steady Cook & a young giddy Housemaid, with a sedate middle aged Man, who is to undertake the double office of Husband to the former & sweetheart to the latter. – No Children of course to be allowed on either side.'

To visit Bath for a short space of time is one thing, but it seems that Jane Austen found the role of dutiful daughter at endless gatherings of older people very dull. They were still observing the outworn social conventions of polite society laid down many years before. Experience may have taught Jane Austen to be somewhat wary of strangers. Her quiet listening posture in some company and a distant manner in later life prompted an unsympathetic observation that she was the most stiff, pernickety, silent spinster ever .

Landsdown Fields, Bath   4 Sydney Place, Bath

Jane Austen certainly had time to observe human nature at its most gregarious and savage in Bath. She came to prefer the role of spectator. She confided to Cassandra how much she disliked parties with a small number of guests. One has to put so much effort into socializing all the time she added.

The countryside is never far away when you are in Bath. The proximity of many interesting and accessible walks must have been a boon to someone who preferred a country life like Jane Austen.

Walking gives an opportunity for conversation or reflection as well as being health giving exercise. It was an antidote to what Jane Austen felt was the *'littleness of town life'* She had enjoyed exploring the countryside round Bath on her previous visits.

Beechen Cliff, The Makers of Bath and The Picturesque

Beechen Cliff must have been a favourite destination for Jane Austen.

'Beechen Cliff, that noble hill whose beautiful verdure and hanging coppice render it so striking an object from almost every opening in Bath.'

Northanger Abbey

Catherine Morland climbs to Beechen Cliff with Henry Tilney and his sister Eleanor. Henry does not seem to have begun with any settled intention of falling in love with Catherine. But her artless admiration has a powerful effect: *'Catherine…enjoyed her usual happiness with Henry Tilney, listening to everything he said; and in finding him irresistible, becoming so herself' Northanger Abbey chapter 16*

From Beechen Cliff there is a view of many of the surviving buildings with which Jane Austen would have been familiar. [Sadly many terraces originally occupied by artisans were destroyed in what is known as 'The Sack of Bath' in the 1960s]

It is said that while the gambler and Master of Ceremonies par excellence Beau Nash had made Bath fashionable, John Wood the Architect and Designer made Bath beautiful, but Ralph Allen made Bath Possible. From a vantage point like Beechen Cliff it is still possible to glimpse the unity of vision for the appearance of the City.

Ralph Allen was a Cornishman, raised by his Grandmother. He came to Bath as a teenager and made two fortunes. The first was through reorganising minor postal routes to be profitable. The money made from this was wisely invested in the stone quarries around Bath

To transport the stone from Combe Down he made a tramway along beside the route of what is still called Ralph Allen's Drive. The marvellous Prior Park is a remarkable achievement of his. It is said he built it to have somewhere a bit quieter than his town house in Lilliput Alley to act as a country retreat, where he could entertain such well known visitors as Alexander Pope. It is also said that another reason was that his Bath stone had just been rejected for the Greenwich barracks. Prior Park was his riposte.

The Oolite limestone, which gives Bath its distinctive honey coloured appearance, is freestone. That is to say the stone does not form in layers, like slate, but can be sawn or 'squared up' in any direction.

So much was taken that in recent times the road above the former quarries on Combe Down was found to be only the thinnest crust with space beneath. A large scheme to fill in the old workings was hastily undertaken.

During much of the eighteenth and early nineteenth century there must have been dust and the noise of construction everywhere in the city.

But here in the pastoral landscape the three young people could admire the view in peace and quiet.

Henry and Eleanor are discussing two concepts. The first is ' the beautiful,' that is to say the harmonious and balanced , such as the designers of Bath were striving to achieve. They obeyed the classical rules in constructing a city where so many buildings are designed please the eye. These edifices show reason and discipline. They are restrained and gracious. It is Greece and Rome reinterpreted for the oolite limestone of the West Country.

The alternative concept is that of 'the picturesque'. Too formal a landscape especially when shown in a painting , might not have the allure of the contrasting idea of 'the picturesque'. Here the rough and romantic, woods, rocks, cliffs and natural features were felt to produce something more mysterious and exciting. It was vital that the representation of the vista fed the imagination.

William Gilpin was a very serious devotee of the picturesque:

'Picturesque beauty is a phrase but little understood. We precisely mean by it that kind of beauty which would look well in a picture. Neither grounds laid out by art nor improved by agriculture are of this kind. The Isle of Wight is in fact, a large garden or rather a field which in every part has been disfigured by the spade, the coulter and the harrow '

This seems a little unrealistic and Gilpin's earnestness of expression idea is taken up and gently mocked by Jane Austen .

In *Northanger Abbey* Catherine is feeling very muddled:

In the present instance, she confessed and lamented her want of knowledge, declared that she would give anything in the world to be able to draw; and a lecture on the picturesque immediately followed, in which his instructions were so clear that she soon began to see beauty in everything admired by him, and her attention was so earnest that he became perfectly satisfied of her having a great deal of natural taste. He talked of foregrounds, distances, and second distances — side–screens and perspectives — lights and shades; and Catherine was so hopeful a scholar that when they gained the top of Beechen Cliff, she voluntarily rejected the whole city of Bath as unworthy to make part of a landscape. Northanger Abbey chapter 14

Gilpin would go even further. Not content with rearranging the view in a painting he suggests taking a mallet to a ruin, in this case Tintern Abbey, to make its appearance more pleasing. Jane Austen makes much the same point, except she is far from serious, when she says that Henry VIII was a benefactor to English Landscape by creating the ruins of the religious houses.

The Cassoon (or Caisson) Lock

Another planned open air excursion was more ambitious. Uncle James Leigh Perrot was an excellent walking companion when he was not lame with gout. In May 1801 Jane Austen speaks warmly of their being able to revive a long held plan to visit the Cassoon Lock.

This was a well-known ramble from Bath at the time, to Combe Hay on the Somerset Coal Canal. The Prince Regent, who became George IV, was shown a demonstration of a caisson lock in April 1799. It was constructed under the supervision of the engineer Robert Weldon, being completed in 1797. It was intended that there should be three such locks,

Each was to be 80 feet long (24.3 metres) and 60 feet (18.2m) deep.

But a soft stratum, probably of fuller's earth meant it was not reliable and the project was abandoned.

The principle is that a narrowboat floats into a sealed watertight box and is raised or lowered between two differing canal levels. It saves all the water necessary for conventional locks.

Boats would move up and down the same pool of 60 feet deep water in the watertight wooden box.

If the ground had been suitable this Georgian engineering feat would have been cheaper to build, saving up to seven conventional locks. It would also save water and move boats faster. No successful commercial example has ever been built. At Combe Hay the lock worked during the demonstration for the Prince Regent. Sixty persons were safely transported. On a subsequent occasion several investors were trapped for some while when a projecting stone jammed the box. The project of the hydrostatical lock was abandoned .

The canal had been intended to bring coal to Bath from the small mining communities of Somerset.

Jane Austen would have been interested in the Kennet and Avon Canal through the connections the Austen family had with the Fowle family at Kintbury. Jane and Cassandra Austen visited the Fowle family regularly. Two sons of Reverend and Mrs Fowle, Fulwar and Tom, were ex-pupils of Mr Austen and Tom was engaged to Cassandra before his early death. Through their friendship with the Fowle family the Austens knew of the Dundas Family who lived at Barton Court nearby and were important in the community. Charles Dundas was Member of Parliament for Berkshire and the Chairman of the Kennet and Avon Canal Company.

Cassandra had received a legacy of £1000 under Tom Fowle's will. In a thoughtful gesture Cassandra left the same amount to an unmarried daughter of the Fowle family in her will to return the compliment.

Jane Austen wrote a little during the time she lived in Bath. She began a novel, The Watsons, which did not go further than about 17,000 words. It concerns a clergyman with poor daughters. Was this situation was too close to her own for dispassionate treatment? Elements were saved. The heroine who lives in Surrey and is called Emma was destined for greater things.. But gentle Emma Watson is all kindness and saves the pride of the spurned child, Charles by offering her hand in the dance without hesitation in an appealing scene. The hopelessness of her situation perhaps made her too tender as a heroine. There are lovely touches of humour. One favourite is Emma's sister who slides away from maternal duties whenever possible. Benign neglect is nothing new it seems, nor insensitive parenting:

'There was a little niece at Croydon, to be fondly enquired after by a kind-hearted Elizabeth, who regretted very much her not being of the party

"you are very good" replied her mother –"and I assure you it went very hard with Augusta to have us come away without her. I was forced to say we were only going to church and promise to come back for her directly"

It is more significant that she was busy revising *Susan (later entitled Northanger Abbey)*, writing a second copy and more than likely incorporating small touches as she observed Bath Society in full flow. In 1803 the copyright was sold through an associate of Henry Austen. Richard Crosby & Company bought it for ten pounds. He did not publish it. Maybe he didn't understand the joke or thought it would damage sales of his gothic high romances. The most important fact is that it was sold. As she had only a few months before refused Harris Bigg-Wither's proposal of marriage it might well have been a much needed boost of confidence for her morale.

Another morale boost, and one of which Cassandra did not

approve was that the gallant Mr Evelyn who Jane Austen describes as horse mad to the exclusion of everything else, made a reappearance. He renewed an acquaintance made during Jane Austen's second family visit to Bath. She very much enjoyed the drives out in his smart Phaeton during the first May of her residency.

Reverend and Mrs Austen would no doubt have looked to their daughters to accompany them and keep them company on occasion. Mrs Austen had a serious illness and required careful nursing. This lady's gratitude is obvious in the verse she wrote about it. The light touch and bantering tone do not disguise the genuine relief and depth of feeling:

Says Death, 'I've been trying these three weeks and more

To seize an old Madam here at Number Four,

Yet I still try in vain, tho' she's turned of three score;

To what is my ill success owing?'
I'll tell you, old Fellow, if you cannot guess,

To what you're indebted for your ill success

– To the prayers of my husband, whose love I possess,

To the care of my daughters, whom Heaven will bless,

To the skill and attention of Bowen

In such a small household Cassandra could not protect Jane and free her to write in the same way as she had before. There must have been a steady flow of social obligations.

The travelling that the Austen family did in these years was extensive, not just further into the West Country, but to friends and relations in many other places. It was not a settled existence.

It may be that she is recollecting her own feelings at this time through Jane Fairfax when she says *"Oh! Miss Woodhouse, the comfort of being sometimes alone!"*

The death of George Austen in January 1805 was a deeply felt bereavement. It also had the consequence of making her totally reliant upon her brothers for food and shelter.

A lifelong friend of the Austen women, Martha Lloyd, who had been nursing her mother through a final illness, now joined their household permanently.

'she really is a friend to all' said Jane Austen.

When she looked back from Clifton, Bristol after a while, Jane Austen commented that they had left Bath *'with what feelings of Happy Escape'*

She never returned.

Holidays by the Sea

Summers can be very trying in the enervating valley where Bath is situated. So the Austen family went travelling, including the famous trips to the Devon and Dorset coast

There is a picture of a female figure with her face hidden executed by Cassandra. This may well be Jane Austen on holiday in the West Country. It is certainly a moment of relaxation and enjoyment. She is seated on what appears to be high ground possibly by the sea. She is certainly looking into the far distance. Her dress is blue; an air of mystery clings to the figure. Her niece,

Anna wrote:

I would give a great deal, that is as much as I could afford, for a sketch which Aunt Cassandra made of her on one of their expeditions-sitting down out of doors, on a hot day with her bonnet strings untied.

Imagine a young woman of twenty five years' old, travelling with her family to Devon and Dorset for the first time. She leans forward in the carriage, bonnet strings untied, eager to see everything. She is ready for her future. It is summertime, 1801. Bath is left behind for a while.

As she travels maybe she muses that during the past five years she has known the pain of losing her sister in law, Anne and also a prospective brother in law, Tom Fowle, who was a childhood friend . Her dear cousin, Jane Cooper (Lady Jane Williams) who survived typhus fever at boarding school with Jane, has died in a riding accident.

Her heart has been touched by a first love, and no doubt severely shaken by the knowledge that her lack of personal fortune affects her marriage prospects.

She is an author who has suffered her first rejection by a publisher, and she has spent the previous few months packing up and dismantling the only home she has known all her life.

But Jane Austen had the resilience of youth and her own natural vitality. Fortitude required past sadness to be set aside. Jane Austen journeyed with her family on an adventure which influenced her future writing profoundly.

As the family caught their first view of the Devon coast with the sun sparkling on the waves, George Austen may well have declaimed 'Thalatta, Thalatta!' (The Sea, The Sea!). This was the shout of joy uttered by 10,000 Greeks. Their campaign against the Persians in 401 B.C. had failed. But to their relief they have reached Mount Theches and can see they are nearing

The Black Sea and safety. Mr Austen would have read the story in *Anabasis* by Xenophon at Oxford. Mrs Austen's reaction might well be to settle herself more firmly beneath her warm travelling blanket against any dampness in the sea air.

I hope you will be able to visualise the County of Devon, with the sunshine shining through the rain which creates this county of rainbows. From her carriage window Jane Austen would have glimpsed the ruby red Devon soil . The main crops of her native Hampshire were wheat, barley, hops and of course the newer turnips. A trend to plant root crops to improve fertility had been spreading from East Anglia. In Hampshire the locals complained that the pigeons who fed on the new turnip crops had lost their former tasty flavour. Both in Hampshire and Devon landowners and gentlemen farmers were showing increasing interest in stock husbandry. Perhaps she could pick out the traditional breeds of sheep with their dense and curly coats which protected them from the West Country storms. The breeds of sheep in Hampshire had springy close wool coats for the Downs which had less rainfall. She could look at livestock with the eye of experience as her Father and Mother used the land which went with their living to be as self- sufficient as possible. Mrs Austen writes with enthusiasm in the early days of her marriage to her sister-in-law, Mrs Walter:

I have got a nice dairy fitted up, and am now worth a bull and six cows, and you would laugh to see them; for they are not much bigger than Jack-asses-and here I have got jackies and ducks and chickens'

Even the famous Devon Reds would not have been bred so large at this time. But an improvement in meat yields meant that London butchers came to prize the Devonian beef cattle.

We know that Jane Austen was very observant as she travelled. The descriptions in *Sense and Sensibility* show that Miss

Austen noted the steep valleys or combes. The pleasing views of woods and fields delighted the eye of this countrywoman. She appreciated that the green and verdant appearance of the county was nurtured by the springs which rose on Dartmoor at its heart. The granite rock, much of which was taken to build important buildings in London, does not allow water to pass into underground waterways. The little streams burble and then tumble in haste down to the sea. The coast was also the destination of the Austen family. They visited resorts in both Devon and neighbouring Dorset in the four years of Mr Austen's retirement.

Jane had foreseen that the proximity of the sea would be an attraction of moving to Bath. She wrote

For a time we shall now possess many of the advantages which I have often thought of with Envy in the wives of Sailors or Soldiers.

Naval and Military wives and families were well known for flocking to the resorts where their menfolk were stationed, and now the Austen family would be the same.

Travelling to the West Country

But what was it like to travel in the days before our many hundreds of miles of motorways? When everything went at the speed of the human foot, donkeys, oxen and horses?

In 1785 it took a mere twenty four hours to travel from London to Exeter. The golden age of coach travel was at its height. The National Trust property at Arlington in North Devon keeps an extensive national collection celebrating this mode of travel.

Travelling in the eighteenth century was arduous and travel sickness not uncommon. The eighteenth century naturalist, Gilbert White could not undertake coach travel without what he delicately refers to as 'cascading'. Eventually he stayed home for the most part. The fruit of his continuance in one place is his masterpiece *The Natural History of Selborne.*

Mrs. Norris, one of the most vicious character creations in Jane Austen's work, only ventures forth for the most important business. In this extract is she at all worried about the horses or the rheumatic coachman ? It seems most likely that she is anxious only to take credit for bringing about Maria's engagement to the extravagantly wealthy but sadly fatuous Mr. Rushworth

'My dear Sir Thomas, if you had seen the state of the roads that day!- though we had the four horses of course-I ached for the old coachman with every jolt .When we got to the bottom of Sandcroft Hill I got out and walked up. I did indeed-I could not bear to sit at my ease and be dragged up at the expense of the noble animals. I caught a dreadful cold but that I did not regard!

People would mostly be carried by private coaches, hired or provided by wealthy relatives or acquaintances. There were also stage coaches which took about six inside passengers and as many as could cling on top of the roof. Jane Austen's nephews, Edward and George, travelled outside by choice when coming to stay at Southampton after the sudden death of their mother. They were allowed beside the coachman, but still not so very comfortable.

Castle Square, Monday October 24, 1808

Edward and George came to us soon after seven on Saturday, very well but very cold, having by choice travelled on the outside, and with no great coat but what Mr Wise, the coachman, good naturedly spared them of his, as they sat by his side.

Mail coaches were fast, no luggage allowed, with a maximum of four passengers. They travelled at about 8 miles per hour. A guard sat next to the driver, armed to repel highwaymen.

In Northanger Abbey the boastful John Thorpe with his open,

one horse gig attempts to impress Catherine Morland! He 'talks it up as curricle hung', but it is really not so fashionable as he would like her to think:

'that horse cannot go less than 10 miles an hour; tie his legs and he will get on. What do you think of my gig, Miss Morland? It was built for a Christ Church man.

Curricle hung, you see; seat, trunk, sword-case, splashing board, lamps, silver moulding all, you see, complete; the iron work as good as new, or better, He asked fifty guineas. I closed with him directly, threw down the money, and the carriage was mine' Northanger Abbey chapter 6

Turnpike trusts (in existence since 1663, but now on the rapid increase) looked after the main routes and levied tolls .Many little toll houses survive and you can sometimes make out the large window on the ground floor where you might pay. In 1815 a heavy wagon with six horses paid two shillings, a coach and four one shilling, and a single horse carriage sixpence. The mail went free. Travellers were given a ticket which might open several gates for several miles along the highway.

About twelve miles was the average distance after which horses must be rested, or changed. As the eighteenth century went on journey times shortened.

The final part of the journey along minor roads was often troublesome, especially in winter. These byways were not commercially maintained. A good example is Lyme Regis where no wheeled traffic could get into the town until 1759, when a turnpike was built. Before that everything was carried by pack horses with wooden boxes or baskets hung each side of their backs. Of course throughout Devon there are still markets known as 'pannier' markets, recalling these former times.

It is no wonder that visits once you arrived were lengthy.

Women did not usually travel alone. This is why there is a truly shocking incident in *Northanger Abbey*.

General Tilney discovers that he has been mistaken in believing Catherine to be wealthy enough to marry his son Henry. He turns her from his house without even enquiring whether she has her fare home. She travels through the night without a servant. It reveals the General to be something of the gothic villain which Catherine Morland is so ashamed to have believed him to be. Luckily she comes to no harm and Henry of course defies his father and proposes marriage immediately!

If bulky items, such as furniture needed to be moved road transport was laborious. When the Austen family moved from Hampshire to Bath, they took only their beds and personal property.

In *Sense and Sensibility* Mrs Dashwood inherits very little as she is a second wife and not mother to the heir. She accepts the offer of a cottage on the estate of her cousin Sir John Middleton in Devon and takes the bits and pieces to which she is entitled. These are taken round by sea from Sussex to Exeter. The new mistress of the house is Fanny Dashwood, grasping wife to Mrs Dashwood's step son John. She grudges the unfortunate widow even her paltry remaining possessions:

The furniture was all sent round by water. It chiefly consisted of household linen, plate, china and books, with an handsome pianoforte of Marianne's. Mrs John Dashwood saw the packages depart with a sigh. She could not help feeling it hard that as Mrs. Dashwood's income would be so trifling in comparison with their own she should have any handsome article of furniture.

The Beginnings of Tourism in Devon and Dorset

The Austen family were following a new trend in visiting the seaside. Visitors had been increasing at a steady rate over the previous twenty years. The following extract shows how fascinating the many small fishing ports and attractive inlets were to city dwellers. They showed a different way of life to people who lived inland. The scenery and fresh air were relished by people who lived in busy, dirty towns.

Fanny Burney watches the fisherwomen of Teignmouth

Fanny Burney was particularly good at describing interesting sights as she travelled. She was somewhat older than Jane Austen and as a successful novelist much admired by Miss Austen, whose name appears in the pre-publication list of subscribers who sponsored the novel *'Camilla'*.

In the following extract, written when Francis Burney was 21 years old she was visiting her step sister, Maria.

Maria had married to Mr. Martin Rishton in 1772. They were living in a cottage by the sea at Teignmouth. It was called Tingmouth at the time.

16th August, 1773

We all went on Monday Evening to the sea shore, to see the scene Drawn: this is a most curious Work: and all done by Women. They have a very long Net, so considerable as to Cost them 13 or 16 pounds – this they first draw into a Boat, which they go off the shore in, and Row in a kind of semi Circle, till they Land at some distance: all the way, they spread this Net, one side of which is kept above Water by Corks. Then they Land, and divide Forces; half of them return to the beginning of the Net, and half remain at the End: and then, with amazing strength, they both divisions , at the same time pull the Net in, by the two Ends: whatever Fish they catch, are always encircled in the middle of the Net, which come out of the Water the last; and, as they draw towards each other, they all join in getting their prey: when once they perceive that there is Fish in their Nets, they set up a loud shout, and make an almost unintelligible Noise, in expressing their joy, and in disputing at the same Time upon their shares, and on what Fish Escaped them. They are all robust and well made, and have remarkably beautiful Teeth; and some of them are really very fine Women: their dress is barbarous: they have stays half Laced, and some thing by way of Handkerchiefs about their Necks, they wear a single coloured Flannel or stuff petticoat; - no shoes or stockings, notwithstanding the hard Pebbles and stones all along the Beach; - and their Coat is Pin'd up in the shape of a pair of trousers, leaving them wholly Naked to the knee.

Mr Western (cousin to F.B's step sister Maria) declares he could not have imagined such a Race of Females existed in a Civilized Country- and had he come hither by sea, he should have almost fancied he had been Cast on a new discovered Coast. They caught, this Evening, at one Time 9 large Salmon, a John Dory, and a Gurnet: on Tuesday Evening we went again, and saw them catch 4 dozen Mackerel at a Haul.

Teignmouth was also an important port in the Newfoundland trade and fisheries, and the women's husbands were now away fishing in Newfoundland. Their strength and enterprise meant they were known as The Amazons after those fearless female hunters.

Scene= seine

One of Jane Austen's favourite poets, William Cowper, wrote of the phenomenon in 1782 in *Retirement*

But now alike, gay widow, virgin, wife

Ingenious to diversify dull life

In coaches, chaises, caravans and hoys,

Fly to the coast for daily, nightly joys

And all, impatient of dry land agree

With one consent, to rush into the sea.

A Change of Air

...'a little fever and indisposition – it has been all the fashion this week at Lyme' –Letter to Cassandra , 4ᵗʰ September, 1804.

Part of the early attraction of coastal visits is explained by the lack of proven medical remedies in the Eighteenth Century. Anything that bolstered health was seized upon with enthusiasm.

In the 1770's a Dr Richard Russell had contributed greatly to the popularity of Brighton after writing a treaty in praise of the beneficial effects of sea water, both drinking it and bathing in it. It was to be the great panacea for CONSTIPATION! Even more joy was visited on the rich and troubled digestive systems by his being the first to recommend CHANGE OF AIR .What delightful promises – REGULARITY and the absolute compulsion and advisability of going away for a good time! Although Dr Russell was both sincere and professional, many others, not so scrupulous rushed to boast the benefits of their attentions.

Jane jokes to Cassandra about the general pre-occupation with health amongst seaside visitors. She says she has recovered from a slight fever and tummy upset well enough to swim. She infers she could not have held her head high amongst the other visitors if she hadn't been slightly under the weather at some time that week. It's just so fashionable to be slightly indisposed.

In Jane Austen's uncompleted final novel the entrepreneur, Mr Parker, is extolling the advantages of a seaside visit:

He held it indeed as certain, that no person could be really well… without spending at least six weeks by the Sea every year.

The Sea air and Sea bathing together were nearly infallible, one or the other of them being a match for every Disorder, of the Stomach, the Lungs or the Blood; They were anti-spasmodic, anti-pulmonary, anti-septic, anti-bilious and anti-rheumatic. Nobody could catch cold by the Sea, Nobody wanted Appetite by the Sea, Nobody wanted Spirits, Nobody wanted Strength – They were healing, softing, relaxing – fortifying and bracing – seemingly just as was wanted – sometimes one, sometimes the other. – If the Sea breeze failed, the Sea-Bath was the certain corrective – and where Bathing disagreed, the Sea Breeze alone was evidently designed by Nature for the cure'

Developers rushed to provide promenades, assembly rooms and terraces of fashionable dwellings on the sea front. They were anxious that visitors should get the full benefit of the sea air and pay generously for that pleasure.

Sea Water Baths

An early reference to sea baths at Sidmouth is made in 1791 . These were referred to in the Exeter Flying Post in June of that

Sea Water Baths, Torquay

Enjoying the Beach at Sidmouth

year as having been erected by Mr Taylor, a Sidmouth Surgeon,

'conveniences for warm sea bathing and the cold shower bath'

Many impressive publications sang their praises:

Dr Land's *'Treatise on the Hot, Cold, Tepid Shower and Vapour Baths'*
While who would ignore a doctor with the name of Ingenhousz
who gave a paper to the Royal Society on *'The Salubrity of the
Common Air at Sea'* in 1780. The sea water baths indeed fulfilled
every requirement.

There was a school of thought that sea bathing should not be at
all enjoyable. The pores must be closed and therefore swimming
at the coldest times of the year was best. Jane's cousin Eliza was
advised that one months' bathing in January would more good
than six months at others times of the year for her invalid son
Hastings. I am sorry to report that he died at the age of fifteen
years.

Chapter Four – Danger and Unrest

The Revolutionary Effect

But there was an overwhelming reason for the growth in popularity of a seaside staycation in this country and that was war with France.

There was one terrible event which eventually led to hostilities. Its consequences prompted a change in the habits of the monied travellers and made them forsake the continent for their native shores.

The event in question had the same impact as the death of Princess Diana, or the assassination of President Kennedy.

Some events are so momentous that their impact imprints itself upon us in an unforgettable way:

Elizabeth Ham, recalling her west country childhood at the age of 66 writes that as a 9 year old:

I remember going into the parlour one day, but this was at Weymouth, and finding my mother and my Aunt Pope in tears. On asking what was the matter, they told me that the wicked French people had cut off the head of their King! Notwithstanding the desperate loyalty of everybody at Weymouth, my anger was most excited against our own King for letting them do it. For I firmly believed the King to be omnipotent. [Diary of Elizabeth Ham]

January 21 1793 Rev. Gilbert White, and author of *The Natural History of Selborne* recorded – *Thrush sings, the song-thrush: the missle-thrush has not been heard. On this day Louis 16th late king of France, was be-headed at Paris, & his body flung into a deep grave without any coffin or funeral service performed.*

Jane Austen's cousin Eliza lost her husband to Madame La Gilloutine the following year.

Military Manoeuvres

'I cried for two days together when Colonel Miller's regiment went away. I thought I should have broken my heart' (Mrs Bennet)

Because of the war with France young men in uniform were suddenly prowling everywhere. Even fashions took on a military flavour, with frogging on short jackets, known as spencers and peaked military style hats.

The removal of the military to winter quarters might bring them to any small town, even Meryton, the fictitious town at the centre of *Pride and Prejudice*

Mrs Bennet makes the best of things:

I remember the time when I liked a red coat myself very well – and indeed, so I do still at my heart; and if a smart young colonel, with five or six thousand a year, should want one of my girls, I shall not say nay to him, and I thought Colonel Forster looked very becoming the other night at Sir William's in his regimentals'

But summertime was spent by the sea, keeping a weather eye out for invasion, whilst impressing the populace with mock battles, drills, marching and firing salutes.

Small wonder that a visit to Brighton

'comprised every possibility of earthly happiness for Lydia.

Henry joined the Oxford Militia, a home defence force called up as required in situations of threat of invasion. The Militia had such camps during the summer in various coastal locations.

They were at Dover Castle in 1803-5, Cornwall in 1807, Gosport, Hampshire 1808 and Littlehampton, near Eastbourne and Chichester in 1809 and 1810.

No doubt at each encampment there were

'tents stretched forth in beauteous uniformity of lines, crowded with the young and gay and dazzling with scarlet'

Henry had hoped to join the 86th and go to the Cape of Good Hope and India . Commissions were commonly bought by families or obtained through influential connections. Training at Woolwich Military Academy must have been expensive. Not having the purchasing power of Fitzwilliam Darcy behind him, as Wickham does, Henry joined the Oxfordshire Militia as a lieutenant, eventually reaching the rank of Captain, becoming an Adjutant and finding sureties to guarantee his credit rating to become a paymaster.

Even the affluent Edward raised the Godmersham and Molash Company of East Coast Volunteers to train and guard the coastline.

Holidays at home became the norm from the declaration of War by France in 1793 . This continued, except for a brief peace for 18 months at the beginning of the nineteenth century. Change only came with the defeat of Napoleon at Waterloo in 1815 . The British seaside was well into its stride and of course, the railways were coming.

The local economy was boosted by coastal garrisons and senior naval officers coming ashore to visit their wives. Naval families stayed nearby the coast .

With Naval involvement both Frances and Charles were called upon to organise the sea fencibles to defend our shores.

Jane Austen wrote with perspicacity about various naval personnel. The kindly Admiral Croft, intelligent and wise, the ne'er do well son of Mr and Mrs Musgrove, the dashing Captain Wentworth and the hard drinking father of Fanny Price. But they earned her admiration, this profession of men who gave their whole lives to that hard mistress, the sea. The naval character is praised in Louisa Musgrove's 'raptures' about the character of the Navy:

..their friendliness, their brotherliness, their openness,; protesting that she was convinced of sailors having more worth and warmth than any other set of men in England

At the time of Jane Austen's visits to Devon and Dorset the British Navy was most closely associated with the West Country through the defence against the threat of invasion.

The news of casualties was frequently disturbing. By 1811 the number of deaths was rising, but the Austens were unaffected.

'How horrible it is to have so many people killed! – and what a blessing that one cares for none of them' A sentiment that makes us wince as we acknowledge its brutal honesty.

Travels in the South West 1801-1804

The details that follow are assembled from such information as we have from letters and hints about Jane Austen's seaside wanderings in the South West

Journeys to Fashionable Resorts in Devon and Dorset

1800	Rev and Mrs. Austen decide to retire to Bath
1801	June to September
	Jane likely visited Sidmouth and Colyton on the Devon coast
1802	Summer visits supposed to Dawlish and Teignmouth
1803	Possibly the Austen family go on holiday to the West Country to the Devon and Dorset coast
	In November the family take an autumn holiday at Lyme Regis.
1804	Midsummer to October- The Austens, in company

with Henry and Eliza Austen holiday on the Devon
and Dorset coast. Later on in the holiday Jane
Austen and her parents stay mainly at Lyme Regis

(List from Paul Poplawski's encyclopaedia)

Sidmouth 1801

J.M.W. Turner travelled extensively in the West Country and
his view of Sidmouth is well known. It seems to capture the
exhilaration of the presence of the ocean. The excitement of the
waves and the changes in the mood of the sea stirred the spirits
of inland dwellers.

Sidmouth was most likely visited by the Austens in 1801.

Politicians seem to like holidaying in the West Country. William
Praed, Member of Parliament, and writer of light verse, sums up
the atmosphere in the early resorts:

The seamen mending sails and oars

The matrons knitting at the doors

The invalids enjoying dips

The children launching tiny ships

The traditional occupations such as fishing continued, while
visitors created a demand for the facilities which they were
used to in resorts such as Bath. They needed a public walkway
for promenading, enjoying the sea air and admiring each other
Tourists also searched for reasonably comfortable lodgings. Jane
Austen does not seem to have been impressed by the standard of
seaside accommodation.

As well as Assembly Rooms for entertainment, shops and
libraries were in demand. In *Sanditon* both needs were met in

one building.

The early stage of the development of Sanditon is immediately obvious by the short list of subscribers to the library and the comment that:

Mrs Whitby at the library was sitting in her inner room, reading one of her own novels for want of employment

But she has used every marketing opportunity and her library obviously sold rings, brooches and other trinkets –

…all the useless things in the world that could not be done without

It is not surprising that they were important centres of social life!

Along the shelves were different categories of reading material: sermons, histories, voyages and travel, tales, novels but no celebrity cooking!.

The growth in popularity of *fiction of fancy* is demonstrated by cartoons of the time. The shelves marked 'novels' and 'romances' were shown as nearly empty, while 'sermons' remain jammed on full shelves! The older generation regarded these new works of fiction with suspicion. In the opinion of many they were probably responsible for the corruption of the young. Every generation has its problems.

In her teenage work, Jane picked up on this in the following snippet:

In Love and Freindship, written when she was in her early teens, Edward and his father are at loggerheads.

'Where Edward in the name of wonder … did you pick up this unmeaning gibberish? You have been studying novels I suspect'.

In the true spirit of youthful rebellion Edward remarks

'Never shall it be said that I obliged my father'

In this gem, one character, Sophia, on point of death, having swooned once too often, advises Laura:

'Run mad as often as you chuse, but do not faint'

Fainting at dramatic points in the story was of course much favoured by the heroines of novels.

As Virginia Woolf remarks

' The girl of fifteen is laughing in her corner, at the world'

Jane's simple formal education ended when she was about eleven, but continued through her father's library of over 500 books and the circulating libraries in places in Bath. There are lots of theories about which writers influenced Jane Austen..

At about the time of Jane Austen's visit, Sidmouth had a well established Circulating Library and Reading Room in a central position, next to Marine Place. It's proud owner, Mr John Wallis produced a town guide, with a panorama insert. This opens to show the Library with its board informing the populace that he also has premises at 42 Skinner Street, London. This must have been to reassure the townsfolk that they were not in an uncivilized backwater.

At the Library and no doubt on your first visit, the purchase of a Guide to the resort was essential.

John Wallis writes in his **1810 *Guide to Sidmouth*:**

'Imperial Rome, in the zenith of her glory, poured forth, every year, her numerous population to the shores of the Adriatic.'

…Within the last forty or fifty years, watering places have been every year more and more the resort of the gay, the idle and the valetudinary'

The reason for this he suggests is to seek

'a frequent renovation of that health which care and business had

impaired, or more frequently, dissipation undermined'

Jane Austen's experience of reading similar publications of flowery prose must have given life to the personality of the founder of the fortunes of the resort of Sanditon, Mr Parker.

Libraries were also important for advertising additional fitness aids, in case a swim and a brisk walk were insufficient. In *Sanditon* Lady Denham is an enterprising lady who has married once for wealth and once for a title. She has managed to keep hold of both. To cash in on any opportunity to make money out of visitors Lady Denham has purchased a piece of gymnasium equipment which was popular at the time and known as a chamber horse.

This was like a giant piano stool, with sturdy springs encased in leather, with handgrips at either side. Depressing the springs with the posterior, their reaction would propel the user into the air. The bouncing motion imitated the trotting gait of horses, a real tonic to the jaded eighteenth system no doubt!

Lady Denham, who herself enjoys perfect health, has instructed Mrs. Whitby, the librarian and centre for tourist information, that :

If anyone enquires for one (a chamber horse), they may be supplied at a fair rate

The development of the resort is obviously bringing out the entrepreneurial spirit in even the local aristocracy.

Colyton - 1801

On the 8th November, 1800 Jane Austen wrote to Cassandra that she had received a friendly letter from Richard Buller and that he is not at all soppy when referring to his wife Anna. This makes her especially well disposed towards him.

He has enquired after all the Austen family and warmly invited them to visit him at Colyton. She sounds pleased that her father is going to take him up on this offer the following summer.

Mr and Mrs Austen had taken in paying pupils for many years. These boys were usually sons of old university friends who needed to be prepared for entrance to Oxford University. Richard Buller was one of these ex-pupils so it must have been a friendly visit, recalling shared times.

Perhaps the party reminisced about the time when Buller and his

Friend Goodenough protested that they could not sleep for the rusty squeak of the rectory weathercock. Mrs Austen helped them by penning a verse to bring it to the Master's attention:

It whines and it groans & it makes such a noise

That it greatly disturbs two unfortunate boys.

Jane Austen must have been intrigued by the history of Colyton.

At the time of Jane Austen's visit, the town was an agricultural market town, with mills, an iron foundry and an oak bark tannery.

It was a community mentioned in the Domesday Book, under the name of Culitone. Miss Austen might have approved of the third code of law issued at Colyton by King Edmund I in about 945. This helped to bring stability to the feudal society by stating clearly its four pillars of

Kingship, Lordship, Family and Neighbourhood. Nothing could better express the established society which Jane Austen esteemed. The themes of settled continuance and the responsibility of the landed classes which appear in Mansfield Park are personified in the steady character and moral purpose of another Edmund, Edmund Bertram.

But I'm sure that she was just as interested to hear of the town's reputation as the most rebellious town in Devon because of the large number of townspeople who joined the Monmouth Rebellion in 1685.

The church still stands, with an outstandingly beautiful lantern tower, said to be used as a beacon for ships on the River Axe, though that may just be a fable. The Vicarage itself was built in 1529.

Although it was a merry meeting, a shadow was hanging over it. Richard Buller was not robust.

Jane mentions him again in 1805 when he comes to Bath to take the waters and is not at all in good health. She writes that he has always had bilious attacks.

Sadly the decline that Jane Austen noted ended with Richard Buller's death the following winter. He was 30 years old. He left Anna and two little children.

Teignmouth- 1802

One of the earliest attractions of Teignmouth in the Eighteenth Century was probably The Amazons of Shaldon, the muscular women who carried on the fishing trade, witnessed by Francis Burney and described elsewhere.

The links with the Northumberland fishing industry remained strong and as they began to wane, the tourist trade took over and as was the trend elsewhere, a Tea House was built on the wide sand dune, now grassy space, amongst the fishing nets.

The sandstone stacks off the shore were traditionally held to be a Bishop of Exeter who was visiting. While he was shown round by a local priest the Devil turned them into two distinct figures, known locally as The Parson and the Clerk.

The town had quickly become fashionable after the French Revolution . In October 1789 The Exeter Flying Post reported that in the courtyard of the Globe Inn at Teignmouth no less than seven coaches with coronets had been sighted together.

Teignmouth was reported to be ;

overflowing with fashionables

The season grew longer and extended into the mild winters. Demand for entertainment grew.

The town had its share of famous residents in the early nineteenth century. There was Thomas Luny, the painter of seascapes, lived in the town from 1807 for thirty years until his death. It is said that he painted over 2,000 paintings while in the town. Charles Babbage (1791-1871) who originated the idea of a programmable computer also lived in the town for some years.

But the person of whom Jane Austen would have had the most knowledge was Edward Pellew, 1st Viscount Exmouth, naval hero, who retired to West Cliff House in 1812

Admiral Edward Pellew retired to Teignmouth as a hero to the men under his command. Of Cornish stock and fond of fighting he ran away to sea at 14, but deserted because of unfair treatment to another midshipman. He proved his gallantry and courage in many actions, quarrelled with a captain, survived captivity and famously commanded and inspired an ill assorted scratch crew of Cornish miners and dozen seamen when appointed to the Nymphe, a 36 gun frigate. This partly trained outfit defeated the French Cleopatre and retrieved a code book of secret signals. Sadly for the French the dying captain had tried to swallow his commission, mistakenly thinking it was the codes.

On 26th January, 1796 the East Indiaman *Dutton*, carrying troops, ran aground under Plymouth Hoe. Pellew, a strong swimmer, took a line out to the wreck and helped rig a lifeline which saved almost all board. As a result he was created a baronet. The sort of elevation so despised by Sir Walter Elliot in *Persuasion.!*

Jane Austen may well have read of such exploits. But the career of Admiral Pellew would have raised some other less welcome reactions than admiration. Jane's fierce loyalty to her siblings would have made for some situations that strained her Christian charity. Admiral Pellew's advancement at the expense of Francis was a good case in point. The situation was this:

Promotion in the Navy relied heavily on patronage which meant one's star rose and fell with the great man to whom one was allied. In the case of Francis Austen this was Lord James Gambier.

Gambier became unpopular. He had many shore appointments 'sailed a desk', as they say. He was well known for a narrow religious outlook – he forced temperance on his men and only allowed married partners aboard. As a result he lost out to action hero Pellew when the Commander in Chief of the Mediterranean Fleet was chosen.

Frank had just secured a wonderful position as Flag-Captain of the *Calendonia* , pride of the Navy, a three decker with 120 guns. This prize was snatched away when she was reassigned from the Gambier to Pellew. After the custom of the day Pellew brought with him his son-in-law to be Flag-Captain, and his brother to be Captain of the Fleet. 'A family ship' was the naval term.

There is genuine anguish as Jane contemplates the future for Francis:

'Henry is convinced that he will have the offer of something else, but does not think it will be at all incumbent on him to accept it; & then follows, what will he do? And where will he live?'.

So Francis had to live with many obstacles to promotion .Brian Southam, brilliant historian and authority on Jane Austen, has pointed out the irony that Admiral Pellew wrote to an unsuccessful officer in terms that might have perfectly fitted Francis's situation:

'you had too many friends of power, who fed your expectations without carrying you over the difficulties every Officer meets in early life'

Francis was an Admiral in late middle age. *In Mansfield Park* Mary Crawford makes an observation:

'I could tell you a great deal; of them and their flags, and the gradation of their pay, and their bickerings and jealousies. But I can assure you that they are all passed over, and all very ill used'

Edward Pellew's life and career were the stuff of legend. We of course have been introduced to him in the character of Captain of *The Indefatigable* portrayed by Robert Lindsay in the television programme *Hornblower*, based on the novels of C.S. Forrester.

Teignmouth was very highly thought of for invalids, including Keats. In Spring 1818 John Keats visited Teignmouth with his brother Tom for several weeks .Tom had succumbed to the family weaknesss for tuberculosis. Keats stayed at 20 Northumberland Street while he was working on his poem *Endymion,* about the shepherd King who is in love with Cynthia, the Moon Goddess. Maybe he had visions of walking the shoreline :

To tread breathless round the frothy main,

And gather up the fancifullest shells

But their arrival coincided with a spell of very wet weather, so Keats wrote to a friend : *the abominable Devonshire weather…the truth is, it is a splashy,rainy,misty,snowy,foggy,haily,floody,muddy,slipshod county*

Shipbuilding and a busy quay (which was away from the areas used by the visitors) made the town profitable. The Quay was built on land leased from Lord Clifford. From 1792 the Stover Canal formed a link to bring ball clay from mines to the north of Newton Abbot to the Quay by long barges which went along the canal then up the estuary. By 1820 the Haytor Granite Tramway was linked to the Stover Canal to bring the granite from Haytor on Dartmoor to build such amazing structures as the new London Bridge.

Dawlish 1802

Dawlish was extremely fashionable in the time of Jane Austen. In her novel

Sense and Sensibility Robert Ferrars, the brother of the hero, cannot believe that the Dashwood womenfolk could or would settle anywhere else in Devon.

Robert Ferrars is the more wordly younger brother of Edward Ferrars who wishes to be a clergyman and marry Eleanor Dashwood. Edward is thwarted in the first ambition by his family's expectations and in the second by the inconvenient fact that while a teenager he became engaged to Lucy Steele, daughter of his Plymouth tutor. Lucy is anxious to keep him to his promise, although eventually she is quick to transfer her affections to Robert when Edward is disinherited for failing to fall in with his mother's wishes.

Elinor is introduced to Robert Ferrars at a musical party in London. She is of course in love with his older brother, Edward, but Lucy Steele has ruined her hopes by telling Elinor in confidence of her secret and longstanding engagement to Edward.Robert opens the conversation politely:

'You reside in Devonshire, I think, in a cottage near Dawlish'

Elinor set him right as to its situation (four miles northward of Exeter)

It seemed rather surprising to him that anybody could live in Devonshire **without** living near Dawlish.

But even if it was not in a prime location, Robert was thrilled that Elinor and her family lived in 'a cottage'. This was a catch all term of the time describing any smaller residence not in the Classical style, but often built with the purpose of entertaining about thirty people to dance and socialize. It might be built as a Romantic flight of fancy, possibly Gothic like Walpole's Strawberry Hill , (mentioned in connection with admission tickets for famous homes later). Often a cottage might be a former farmhouse modernised and provided with a verandah and bay windows , as envisaged by Jane Austen when she describes the house of Charles and Mary Musgrove in Persuasion. It would be thought of as rather and smart and up to minute. Twickenham, where Walpole bought the last plot with a river frontage, would be the dream location as you can tell from Robert's rhapsody to Elinor:

For my own part I am excessively fond of a cottage; there is always so much comfort, so much elegance about them. And I protest, if I had any money to spare, I should buy a little land and build one myself, within a short distance of London, where I might drive myself down at any time and collect a few friends about me and be happy.

My friend, Lord Courtland, came to me the other day on purpose to ask my advice, and laid before me three different plans of Bonomi's*. I was to decide on the best of them. My dear Courtland' said I, immediately throwing them all into the fire' do not adopt either of them, but by all means build a cottage.

Elinor agreed to it all , for she did not think he deserved the compliment of rational opposition.

Barton Cottage is far from convenient.

*a fashionable Italian architect and draughtsman of the time.

It's worth mentioning that the rogue Willoughby in *Sense and Sensibility* also joins in the romantic chorus of praise for cottage as being is *the only form of building in which happiness is attainable.*

At the conclusion of the novel fashionable Dawlish is the natural choice of honeymoon destination for Robert Ferrars and Lucy Steele.It suits a social climber married to a dilettante very well.

They passed some months in great happiness in Dawlish; for she had a great many relations and old acquaintance to cut – and he drew several plans for magnificent cottages

Although Dawlish might be popular, Jane Austen had her own throwaway assessment of its amenities which has become famous. Her niece submitted some writing for her aunt's appraisal. Aunt Jane replied in a letter written on Wednesday 10th to Thursday 18th August 1814. The length and detail of what the famous authoress says both show how painstaking she was as to accuracy. She explains to Anna that she thinks the description of Dawlish is accurate. But she jokes that the Library was absolutely hopeless when she had visited twelve years ago and it wasn't possible to get anything decent to read there.

I am not sensible of any blunders (you have made) about Dawlish. The Library was particularly pitiful & wretched 12 years ago, & not likely to have anybody's publication

Dawlish did not have the same industrial interests as Teignmouth. It grew in a different way after the railway was built along the site of the Promenade. This led to the development of Dawlish Warren as a destination for holiday makers, just outside the old town.

1803 and 1804 - Lyme Regis

Jane Austen's interest in the naval profession began when her brothers both went off to naval college and then to sea. Lyme Regis is associated with her admiration for their profession, which began when she was much younger.

In her early work, known as the *Juvenilia* because it was written when Jane Austen was very young, she writes a short story for her brother, Francis, then a naval midshipman.

The Adventures of Mr. Harley

A short, but interesting tale, is with all imaginable Respect inscribed to Mr Frances William Austen Midshipman on board his Majesty's Ship the Perseverance by his Obedient Servant – The Author.

Mr Harley was one of many Children. Destined by his father for the Church and by his Mother for the Sea, desirous of pleasing both he prevailed on Sir John to obtain for him a Chaplaincy on board a Man of War. He accordingly cut his Hair and sailed.

In half a year he returned and set-off in the Stage Coach for Hogsworth Green, the seat of Emma. His fellow travellers were, A man without a Hat, Another with two, An Old maid and a young Wife.

This last appeared about 17 with fine dark eyes and an elegant shape; in short Mr. Harley soon found out that she was his Emma and recollected that he had married her a few weeks before he left England

Finis.

Lyme Regis is closely identified with Jane Austen. In her final completed novel, *Persuasion*, the plot turns upon a visit to Lyme.

The cheaper cost of living to be found in places like Lyme, as well as its proximity to the Fleet in Plymouth, made it a popular place for retirement and lodgings of sailors. Sailors were of course on half pay during times of peace.

Some were like Captain Harville *in Persuasion*, who

…'had taken his present house for half a year; his taste, and his health, and his fortune, all directing him to a residence unexpensive, and by the sea.

Tradition holds that Jane Austen based the character of Harville upon her brother Francis. Certainly they are both described as being good natured and able to turn their hands to anything. Certainly in one of the earliest surviving letters from Jane to her sister Cassandra Jane praises his skill in wood turning for he has made a miniature butter churn for his little three year old niece Fanny:

Thursday 1st September, 1796

Frank has turned a very nice little butter churn for Fanny.

Fanny's affectionate and skilful Uncle Francis was twenty two years old.

Lyme comes into the plot of *Persuasion* when Captain Frederick Wentworth decides to visit his old shipmate, Captain Harville, who is living there.

Captain Frederick Wentworth, a wealthy bachelor with prize money from his successful naval career, is minded to marry.

He is still nursing a grievance from Anne Eliot's rejection ten years before, when they were very young. This did not spring from want of feeling on her part, but upon the advice of her deceased Mother's friend, Lady Russell. He had only prospects at this time and not proved success or a fortune.

He is now taken with the lively Louisa Musgrove.

Captain James Benwick, mourning his dead fiancée, Fanny Harville, is a member of the household. He is Harville's brother-in-law. The visiting party comprises the Musgroves - Louisa and her sister Henrietta, Charles and Mary and Mary's sister Anne.

The famous Cobb at Lyme made a deep impression on Jane Austen. It must have appealed to her sense of the dramatic:

'the principal street, almost hurrying into the water, the walk to the Cobb, skirting round the pleasant little bay, which in the Season is animated with bathing machines and company, the Cobb itself, its old wonders and new improvements.

The Cobb is the setting for Louisa Musgrove to run up the steps and jump into Captain Wentworth's arms. Granny's teeth is a popular choice for the scene, although the area is much changed .

Louisa slips from Captain's Wentworth's grasp and falls unconscious. Her slow recovery in Lyme gives ample opportunity for her to transfer her affections to cheer up the mournful James Benwick, leaving the field clear for Wentworth to court Anne. But oh dear, here is William Elliot on the scene, appraising Anne, who now has roses in her cheeks from the sea air and is looking better. Complications abound.

Jane Austen's descriptions of Lyme and its surroundings are something special in her work. They are personal and written from the heart:

A very strange stranger it must be , who does not see charms in the immediate environs of Lyme, to make him wish to know it better. The scenes in its neighbourhood, Charmouth, with its high grounds and extensive sweeps of country, and still more, its sweet, retired bay, backed by dark cliffs, where fragments of low rock among the sands make it the happiest spot for watching the flow of the tide, for sitting in unwearied contemplation…

To a society nourished on the traditions of classical beauty and proportion, and the romantic visions of landscape created by Brown, Kent and Repton the natural beauty of the coastline was a fresh revelation.

The hillside setting of Lyme meant the town had a natural defence in the English Civil War, when it was controlled by the Parliamentary forces. They were able to hold out against a Royalist siege of two months. Visitors to Lyme, such as the Austen family, would have read about this *'obstinacy of defence'* in publications such as *'Picture of Lyme Regis and its Environs'* . The confrontation is famous for the role of the womenfolk who bravely joined and loaded muskets. They wore red to make the defence force appear more numerous.

In 1803 after a possible touring visit to Devon and Dorset resorts, the famous sunny Novembers that Lyme Regis enjoys found the Austen family party there, and they stayed at Lyme Regis again in 1804, when they toured the Devon and Dorset coast . There is also a plaque on Pyne House at the bottom of the Broad Street, identifying it as a likely lodging house for the Austen family.

A letter dated 14th September, 1804 is Jane Austen's only surviving letter from her West Country visits to the sea. It covers such familiar situations as a breakage in the holiday home.

I have written to Mr Pyne, on the subject of the broken lid;-it was valued by Anning here, w are told, at five shillings, & as that appeared to us beyond the value of all the furniture in the room together, we have referred ourselves to the Owner.

Anning is the family name of Mary Anning, who with her brother found and sold 'curiosities', fossils which abound in the cliffs round Lyme Regis. This reference is probably to her father, Richard, who was a carpenter in the town at the time. Nowadays her pioneering work in uncovering fossilised remains is celebrated everywhere, not least in the street furniture, where the street lights sport a graceful wrought iron ammonite in the curve of each lamppost.

The letter gives a very full impression of the pastimes essential to a stay at Lyme. Jane Austen makes the acquaintance of a Miss Armstrong, a good walking companion. When Jane pays a call on her , she is taken aback by the fact that: *Her mother was repairing stockings all the time I was there.* She asks Cassandra not to tell their mother, in case she thinks this is a good idea and adopts the habit when callers come. Such a display of lack of sophistication would shock her daughters of course. In Jane Austen's letter an evening event at the Assembly Room is described . An aggravating young man spends the time watching her, then asks for a dance just as she was leaving; how provoking. Jane Austen also mentions that Mr Austen returned to their lodgings with James the manservant. It was such a clear moonlit night that they had no need of the new lantern. James is mentioned as a valued member of the household. It is interesting that Jane Austen is encouraging James the manservant in his reading by passing on the newspaper to him.

The Assembly Rooms were built beside the water and jutting out over it with windows on three sides, so light and airy that Constance Hill, on her literary pilgrimage to places associated with Jane Austen, is effusive in her description. It appeared to be nearly afloat, she claimed. It was the work of Thomas Hollis, the developer of the town. The magic he wrought on the port and fishing community, making it attractive to visitors, seems to suggest the seeds of an idea later realised in the exuberant Mr Parker of *Sanditon.*

The perfect seaside stay would not be complete without sea bathing.

A little sea bathing would set me up for ever' – Mrs Bennet, Pride and Prejudice

The bathing machines were huts on wheels, stationed on the shore in segregated areas for men and women. Bathers entered the huts to prepare themselves. Clothing was worn, though in nearly every print a gentleman may be observed with a spy glass, looking at a naked female bather. Buxom ladies 'skinny dipping' are widely portrayed to satisfy the wishful thinking of male visitors.

The bathing hut was wheeled out into the sea, either dragged or pulled by horses or donkeys, who were then unhitched and taken back to shore

Attended by a maid, or one of the 'dippers', women assistants – some of whom became quite famous favourites, it was possible to descend into the water directly from the bathing machine

From the tone of Jane Austen's letter one can gather the slight element of risk that gave sea bathing its excitement. She stays in too long, there are **CONSEQUENCES**

'The Bathing was so delightful this morning and Molly so pressing with me that I believe I staid in rather too long, as since the middle of the day I have felt unreasonably tired. I shall be more careful another time, and shall not bathe tomorrow, as I had before intended"

At least Jane did not have the experience of George III when sea-bathing at Weymouth after his recent bout of ill health. The King emerged from his bathing machine and entered the briny. As he descended cautiously into the water a band ,hidden in an adjacent bathing machine, struck up God Save the King!!!

There surely cannot be many post boxes to rival the one in Lyme. Thanks are due to Maggie Lane for her excellent study of Lyme Regis with a photograph showing the two slits, one for the convenience of those on horseback, another for those who took letters to the box on foot.

On holiday, as at home, letter writing was a solace, distraction and necessity of daily life. It does not escape Jane's savage humour:

John Knightley is concerned that Jane Fairfax has got wet collecting her post.

'The Post Office has great charm at one period in our lives. When You

have lived to my age, you will begin to think letters are never worth going through the rain for.'

There was a little blush

'I cannot expect that simply growing older should make me indifferent about letters.

'Indifferent! Oh! No-I never conceived you could become indifferent. Letters are no matter of indifference; they are generally a very positive curse'

'You are speaking of letters of business; mine are letters of friendship'

'I have often thought them the worst of the two,' replied he coolly. 'Business, you know, may bring money, but friendship hardly ever does'. Emma ch 34

In Exeter letters must be put in by 6.30, or between 6.30 and 7 an extra penny must be paid. They took about 2 days to London. If only things had improved in two hundred years.

When Mr and Mrs Austen went to the Devon and Dorset coast in 1804 they toured with Jane's favourite brother Henry and his wife, Eliza before settling at Lyme Regis, while Jane Austen kept house for her parents.

Jane herself is remembered in a charming garden, recently replanted, which is terraced on the hill above the walk to the Cobb.

Maybe one day the bust of our heroine, which mysteriously disappeared in the recent past, will be replaced to gaze out at the shining sea once again.

The continuing existence and improvement of this garden is thanks to the effforts of the local authority at Lyme. They have been supported and encouraged by the advice and expertise of distinguished local resident, Diana Shervington and the inspiration of her daughter Caroline, a professional gardener.

Mrs Diana Shervington is a direct descendant of Jane Austen. She has been the valued First President of the local South West Branch of the Jane Austen Society and has entranced a new generation by her delightful memories. She herself is an artist and a professional potter.

Royal visits to Weymouth

'wherever one of the queen bees of fashion alights, a whole swarm follows after'

Jane Austen makes a reference to Gloucester House in her letter of 1804. It is a slightly scathing mention of the Royal Family. Cassandra has gone to Weymluth. Jane is keeping house and looking after her parents..

George III visited Weymouth and Plymouth for the first time in 1789 and returned nearly every year thereafter, until the return of his misunderstood malady, porphyria which kept him confined and lonely for many of his later years.

After taking the air and bathing in the sea on this occasion however George III was restored to *'full health and joyous spirits'*, an happy circumstance that did more than any other factor to popularize the seaside

There are many well-known accounts of these visits by courtiers such as the diarist Fanny Burney. But there is also a very interesting plebeian voice .Elizabeth Ham was destined to fulfil all the uncomfortable destiny of the eighteenth century woman who did not marry and was forced by financial circumstance into the life of a governess. Her wistful observation on youth is something of which Jane Austen makes us poignantly aware.

Elizabeth Ham is of the stated opinion that

'We live a large portion of our lives between fifteen and twenty-five'

Poor Elizabeth, she found life very hard going after that happy West Country Girlhood. Elizabeth was the daughter of a yeoman farmer and brewer to whom King George took a particular liking, comments with a special freshness on the visits from the point of view of an enthralled young person. She was in Weymouth in 1804.

'It was always a gay and joyful day when they came. The troops drawn up in line, and all the inhabitants and visitors on the Esplanade waiting to welcome them'

She reports the six horses pulling each carriage, the shouts, bands, volley of ceremonial salute and the evening grand illumination.

'We all breathed loyalty from the very air of the place'

Princess Amelia was particularly remembered:

'She was not much older than myself, and, when I first saw her descend from the carriage, was nursing a doll'.

Elizabeth records how hordes of friends and relations would descend on them, begging to share beds so they could see the Royal Family.

The King sought out Elizabeth's father to catch up on the local news, embarrassed him by commissioning some sheep for his farm in Windsor for which payment was never received, and in the loud voice for which he was famous announcing one time:

'Mrs. Ham was decidedly the finest woman in Weymouth' You can almost hear him adding his famous *'what what'*

The high spirits and enjoyment of these reminiscences is infectious, recalling the weekly sailing parties of the Royal

Family There is the atmospheric mention of the tense moment of an invasion scare. The French Fleet were thought to be lurking offshore in a thick fog. Elizabeth saw all the carriages standing at the ready outside Gloucester Lodge, prepared to be away in a heartbeat if danger threatened. One can imagine the soft jingle and stamp of the horses, their noise muffled by the murky sea air as thy wait prepared to be away if danger loomed.

Of course the Naval Officers played their part in her memories and in particular water parties:

'..Of all visiting, these parties on ship-board were then the most delightful. The little anxiety about the weather enhanced the pleasure of a fine day, then the excitement of getting on board.

There was something particularly exhilarating in the long, well timed sweep of the eighteen-oared barge over the dancing waters, then the blue coated beaux, wrapping boat cloaks and bunting round the ladies feet. Then being tucked in the commodious chair to be hoisted on board, when timid young ladies used to affect still more timidity than naturally belonged to them

The weather was propitious, the barge waiting for us. The deck of the ship converted into a Saloon for dancing by means of tarpaulin lined with flags. By striking away the stanchions between decks a good spring was given to the floor, considered a great advantage in the spirited jumping days of Country Dances. The cool sea breezes made these temporary Ball-rooms quite delightful and refreshing, very different from the pent-in atmosphere of a closed room on shore'.

In *Emma* a near catastrophe at Weymouth when Jane Fairfax was about to fall overboard mirrors a real life incident reported by Elizabeth. Too impetuous and proud to engage a pilot, the young naval officers had set off for a picnic on the island of Herm. Hitting the rocks the boat sprang a leak – *'each sailor was baling out the water with his hat. Each of the Officers had at least two ladies clinging to him'*

They were rescued by a nearby Mackerel boat *'I seem even now to feel the sensation of treading on slippery fish'* A second boat which had anxiously witnessed the whole affair had been alerted by one of the sailors starting with an oath exclaiming *' we must have a swimming match for the ladies!'*

All good things must come to an end, even holidays by the sea.

Even the departure of the Royal Family is described by the clear recall of Elizabeth:

'Too soon this delightful season came to an End' The Royal Family departed, the protecting Frigates fired their last salute and bore away, emerging from their cloud of smoke with their glorious clouds of canvas all set to catch the breeze. It was a beautiful night, for the spring tide allowed of their sweeping in near the shore and tacking in simultaneous order, their white sails catching the rays of the setting sun. It was once of those pictures that remain stereotyped in the memory. Our visitors departed with our gaieties.'

Chapter Five – Great Houses

Visiting Great Houses

Visiting stately homes is by no means a modern craze. In the Eighteenth Century the wonderful modern country houses were constructed on profits from colonial possessions. They were filled with collections of fine art and expensive and rare objects amassed by men who had vast fortunes at their command. The gardens and parkland surrounding these properties were reconfigured by 'Improvements' were made under the direction of such landscape gardeners as William Kent, Capability Brown and Humphrey Repton

One of Jane Austen's preferred poets, Cowper, was very scathing of Capability Brown in his poem *'The Task'* :

Improvement, the idol of the age,

Is fed up with many a victim. Lo! He comes-

The omnipotent magician, Brown, appears

He speaks. The lake in front becomes a lawn.

Woods vanish, hills subside, and valleys rise,

And streams as if created for his use,

Pursue the track of his directing wand

Lancelot Brown was well known for his engineering abilities. He was an excellent surveyor and had a thorough appreciation of the requirements of the landowners who employed him. They required a wide canvas and facilities to pursue hunting, shooting fishing. The old formal gardens must go. In the interests of sweeping approaches it was unfortunate that often whole villages were moved , watercourses diverted and landscape completely sculpted. Mature trees were introduced, the ancient trees we now see on his estates were saplings which would eventually provide shady walks and arbours near the house so ladies could take exercise.

But even a partial list of properties Brown worked on in the West Country generates a respect for his industry: Savernake Forest, Lacock Abbey, Bowood House, Longleat, Stourhead, and Corsham Court in Wiltshire; Prior Park, Kelston and Newton Park in Somerset; Milton Abbey in Dorset, Mamhead, Widdicombe (Slapton) and Ugbrooke in Devon.

Humphrey Repton who followed Brown was perhaps more artistic and sensitive in his approach He was a talented painter who demonstrated his proposals with 'before and 'after' pictures and overlays. But the grandiose plans of Mrs Austen's cousin, Rev. Thomas Leigh of Adelstrop, the work undertaken by Repton in Gloucestershire and his further proposals for Stoneleigh Abbey may have made her Jane Austen uneasy. In Mansfield Park this apprehension is expressed by Fanny Price's concern over the felling of an avenue of trees. When Mr Rushworth speaks enthusiastically of employing Mr Repton's services Lady Bertram stirs herself to interject:

If I were you I would have a very pretty shrubbery. One likes to get out into a shrubbery in fine weather.

Jane Austen was very interested in this notion of 'improvement'. But it seemed to sometimes be achieved at the expense of destroying some of the best of what had gone before.

In the West Country, however Repton was extremely pleased with what he managed to create at Anthony in Cornwall, and took the trouble to present his red leather bound books of plans and pictures to George III to show him the transformation.

Visitors to such places as Stowe in Buckinghamshire appreciated, admired and also come away with ideas they could adapt for their own properties. Visits were usually arranged by applying to the housekeeper, but in some places the demand was so great that numbers had to be monitored.

One very famous house was Strawberry Hill at Twickenham. It caused a sensation for its gothic architecture and the collections gathered with exquisite taste by its owner, Mr Horace Walpole .

Of course in the novel *Mansfield Park* the delights of Twickenham are obviously well known to Mary and Henry Crawford. Mary speaks lightly of the inconvenience of living with their uncle's improvements to his new property there. It is also while staying with racy friends in this fashionable location that Maria Bertram becomes fatally re-acquainted with the amoral Henry Crawford. This infatuation results in her elopement and betrayal. The beau monde would delight in a weekend of gambling and flirtation. A little licentious behaviour out of Town provided the newspapers with gossip such as that relished by Fanny Price's father. He reads of his niece's downfall comfortably in his slummucky home in Portsmouth no doubt over a pint of ale, and an ounce of tobacco.

Horace Walpole eventually retreated to his cottage in the flower garden emerging only for special visitors. He relied on his housekeeper, Mrs. Ann Bransom to show others around. He developed a system of ticketing and a set of rules:

Mr Walpole is very happy to oblige any curious persons with the sight of his house and collections, but as it is situated so near to London and in so populous a Neighbourhood, and as he refuses a Ticket to nobody who sends for one, it is but reasonable that such Persons as send should comply with the Rules he has been obliged to lay down for showing it.

Mr Walpole goes on to explain he will issue tickets to four people, and four only at a time, for specific days. Visitors may be admitted between the hours of Midday and Three before Dinner, from the First of May to the First of October.

He sternly concludes:

They who have tickets are desired not to bring children.

Although Horace Walpole printed special tickets in 1744, he usually just wrote notes in reply to requests sent to him at Strawberry Hill or Berkeley Square. After 1784 these were typically written on the printed list of rules. These rather bossy notes were given to rich and influential people, who seem to have been happy to obey the rules.

The grand Panton family, for instance, had a street in London, near St Martin's in the Fields, which bears their name. But their origins were as chancers; the seventeenth century founder of the family's property fortune was described as 'a gambler'. They complied meekly with 'the Rules' and kept the ticket as a souvenir.

Mr Panton's ticket has survived at the Louis Walpole Library of Yale University. It is written at the bottom of a rule list:

June 24th 1784

To Mr Walpole's Housekeeper,

You may show My House on Friday morning next to Mr Panton and Three more, on their delivering this to you,

Hor. Walpole

Horace Walpole referred to Strawberry Hill as 'a little plaything house, a little rural bijoux'. We have our own such residence in Devon. It is known as A La Ronde and was built above Exmouth in the 1790's by Mary and Jane Parminter. They had undertaken their own Grand Tour and were inspired by the octoganal Basilica of San Vitale at Ravenna. It was a tribute to feminine taste and ingenuity. It is possible to follow the sun through the day by moving from room to room. For two hundred years all its owners were women.

Powderham Castle, Devon.

Sir Philip Courtenay began building Powderham Castle beside the estuary of the river Exe in 1391. Today the same family lives there and it is currently the home of the 18th Earl and Countess of Devon.

It has a deer park which being only permitted by the Monarch, is a true indication of the long held tenure of an ancient family. Mansfield Park is of course a modern home, built upon the profits of colonial possessions and slavery, though Mary Crawford notices that it does have a substantial park of 'five miles round'.

When we choose to visit a house owned by a private family or run by the National Trust we are at least sure of our welcome . In the Eighteenth century it was often possible to tour a house upon application to The Housekeeper, as happens in *Pride and Prejudice.* Elizabeth Bennet and The Gardiners are received cordially by Mrs Reynolds at Pemberley, not to mention its owner, Mr Darcy, who arrives unexpectedly much to Elizabeth's confusion!

But one poor Mrs. Price, from Bath, writes of a plainly embarrassing experience at Powderham Castle. She mistimes her visit. The Earl is in residence. He is not anxious to receive members of the public.

The housekeeper acting on orders from Lord Courtenay turned them away:

She writes indignantly in her diary:

I then begged to be allowed to drive to the front of the house and through the grounds, but that also was refused....we came away without seeing one thing but the back of the house..... we also saw his Lordship cross the yard, he came past the carriage, but he never turned his head to look at us, feeling conscious I suppose how illiberally he had treated us .. I really felt very much hurt and mortified at my disappointment

Berry Pomeroy Castle

Dawlish in Georgian times

Sadly there was no romantic encounter in the grounds for Mrs Price. Elizabeth and her Uncle and Aunt Gardiner are more fortunate!

Saltram House, Plymouth, Devon , became famous for its 'very choice and expensive collection of pictures', so maybe it also attracted many visitors. In modern times it has certainly featured as Norland Park in both the 1996 and 2007 adaptations of the story *Sense and Sensibility*, which has made sure it is still a very popular place to visit.

Many of the paintings were bought on the advice of the Devon born artist Joshua Reynolds. He was not from an aristocratic background and benefited from the patronage of local wealthy and important families like the Parkers of Saltram. He spent a great of time joining in leisure pursuits at the house and painted many members of the family. He recommended to the second Lord John Parker and his wife Therese where the purchased paintings could best be hung in the remodelled house.

Sir Joshua died in London in 1792, in his sixty ninth year. He was England's foremost portrait painter. In 1813 Jane Austen went to a major exhibition of his work held at The British Institution, while staying with her brother Henry.

At the time Jane Austen was enjoying herself in a daydream of how Jane Bennet and Elizabeth Bennet would look as young wives.

Henry and I went to the Exhibition in Spring Gardens. It is not thought a good collection, but I was very well pleased-particularly (pray tell Fanny) with a small portrait of Mrs. Bingley .....She is dressed in a white gown with green ornaments, which convinces me of what I had always supposed, that green was a favourite colour with her. I dare say Mrs D. will be in yellow.

When Jane Austen does not find a portrait to chime with her imagination of how Elizabeth Darcy would look at either The Great Exhibition or the Exhibition of Sir Joshua Reynolds' paintings, she is philosophical.

I can only imagine that Mr D. prizes any picture of her too much to like it should be exposed to the public eye-I can imagine he would have that …. Mixture of Love, Pride & Delicacy.

Of course Jane Austen had a direct link with Saltram herself through an acquaintance with Frances Morley. This interesting lady was the daughter of a Norfolk surgeon, Mr Talbot. She married John Parker of Saltram and became Lady Boringdon. In 1815 he was elevated to the Earldom of Morley and she became a Countess.

It was a somewhat remarkable marriage to make

John Parker, 1st Earl of Morley, 1772-1840 was known as Borino in his younger days (as being a play on 2nd Lord Boringdon) His first wife, Lady Augusta Fane eloped with Sir Arthur Paget. Despite this disappointment and scandal, Frances Talbot accepted his somewhat offhand proposal.

Lady Granville commented

'Were you surprised at Lord Boringdon's marriage? Miss Talbot is a most delightful person, extremely pretty and agreeable. How they all do surprise me by accepting him. I do not envy his wife and happy in my mind was she who ran'

He certainly lived extravagantly and had relationships with other women, notably Lady Elizabeth Monck daughter of Earl of the Arran who bore him three sons. But everyone shook down together and one of these boys Augustus Stapleton, became the Prime Minister Cannings' private secretary and executor of his father's will.

Frances Morley made a pragmatic success of this difficult domestic situation. She had a reputation as an intelligent wit. In fact it was rumoured that she was the writer of *Sense and Sensibility and Pride and Prejudice*. Frances Morley was not exactly quick to deny she was the author of these popular works! The books had been published as being *By a Lady* to preserve Jane Austen's anonymity. We do not know how these two accomplished ladies were introduced, but we imagine that they met through Henry Austen's wide circle of acquaintance. Jane sent Frances Morley a copy of *Emma* in December *1815*, and received a very civil reply. Here are two brief extracts, both exhibiting extravagant politeness.

I have been most anxiously waiting for an introduction to Emma........ I am already become intimate in the Woodhouse family & feel they will not amuse & interest me less than the Bennetts, Bertrams Norris & all their admirable predecessors-I can give them no higher praise- I am Madam, Yr much obliged F.Morley

Jane Austen replied gracefully and modestly:

...It is particularly gratifying to receive so early an assurance of your Ladyship's approbation. It encourages me to depend on the same share of general good opinion which Emma's predecessors have experienced, and to believe that I have not – as almost every writer of fancy does sooner or later – overwritten myself.

I am Madam   Your obliged and faithful servant J. Austen

Set-Jetting in the West Country

At the conclusion of a film in a cinema many of the audience jump up and leave quickly.

But some always linger to the very end of the film credits, stretching their legs , while their eyes are fixed to the screen for the soundtrack titles and the location acknowledgements. For some it is a fascinating aspect of film-making.

Where was it filmed? This question is a complicated one to answer, with the interior of this building and the exterior of another used. A whole range of geographical choices are examined before decisions are made.

So what I give here is a small selection of West Country places which you may know or come across on a day out. Others have created more definitive guides.

Sense and Sensibility, drafted first in 1795 , has a Devonian setting for part of its story. Film makers have used a wide range of locations throughout the south west . Trafalgar House in Wiltshire features as Barton Park, Devon. There is also a glimpse of Compton Castle. In 1995 Efford House on The Flete Estate was transformed into Barton Cottage. It's magical situation made the most of the beautiful coastline and estuary. We have already mentioned Saltram . Wilton House in Salisbury forms the setting for the London Ball where Marianne surprises Willoughby . Chandos House and a house in Adam Street are the London homes of the Palmers and the Dashwoods. Mompesson House in Salisbury takes a role as Mrs Jennings London Home.

On her way home to take refuge in Devon the wonderful grounds of Montecute House near Yeovil are where the sad Marianne wanders and catches her life threatening fever.

Finally happiness reigns as Marianne and Colonel Brandon are finally married at the little church of Berry Pomeroy. I hope they got on alright, in spite of his being thirty five and so very old and decrepit according to Marianne! The flannel waistcoat of which he is glad sounds practical in view of the Devon climate! The screenplay for this film was written by Emma Thompson.

In 2007 the talented Andrew Davies, who has dramatized many classic novels, wrote the screenplay for the BBC 's version of the story. This time Saltram could not be bettered as Norland Park.

At Hartland Abbey in North Devon the fifteenth century Blackpool Mill Cottage on the estate, owned by Sir Hugh and Lady Angela Stucley is Barton Cottage.

Sharp eyed devotees may spot Clovelly Pier, and Dyrham Park featuring as Allenham. Other locations are in the Home Counties.

Persuasion

The 1995 version of Persuasion and the 2007 adaptation both make extensive use of locations in the City of Bath. Royal Crescent, the Assembly Rooms, Abbey Churchyard, Old Bond Street, Bath Street and Abbey Green are all central.A gracious house in Sydney Buildings , which takes the part of Sir Walter Elliot's house in Bath, is at the end of Great Pulteney Street. The famous George Inn at the village of Norton St Philip near Bath is used for the accommodation at Lyme where the party glimpse William Eliot and his splendid carriage.

Perhaps two locations used in Bath have become so iconic that they deserve a special mention. The first is the Colonnades in Bath Street.

Captain Wentworth has declared himself by letter. Anne and he have finally come to an understanding. After the custom of modern day filming they are permitted to embrace. The kiss takes place under the archway. As they stand lost in the rediscovery of their enduring love a circus procession passes by. Bath is all about theatrical show and display. The reality of their feelings is in direct contrast to its tawdry artifice.

Captain Wentworth now escorts Anne back to Camden Place. But rather than walk directly up Lansdown Hill he takes her the long way home, going by way of The Gravel Walk, which leads from Queen's Parade to Royal Crescent and Upper Church Street. Even today it has the reputation as a romantic spot.

Out in Wiltshire Sheldon Manor at Chippenham is Upper Cross Great House. Neston Park at Corsham is Kellynch Hall (2007) Seaton, Dorset is Lyme.

In the 1995 adaptation Barnsley Park is Kellynch Hall, Sheldon Manor is Uppercross, Lyme appears as itself and some scenes are from Portsmouth.

The Puzzle of Barton

Did Jane Austen have a specific location in mind when she created the village of Barton in Devon for her novel *Sense and Sensibility?*

In her work such well known places as Bath, London, Brighton, Ramsgate, Weymouth and Lyme Regis appear as themselves. They were all distinctively well-known at the time. But smaller places such as Highbury in *Emma* or Meryton in *Pride and Prejudice* are dear to us because they are typical. So much seems to have been generally accepted and particular places have rarely been associated with these presumably fictional creations. It would seem logical to place Barton in this category had it not been for those six words *within four miles northward of Exeter.* It has just that tantalising suggestion of the specific which sparks fearsome investigation and scrutiny of every geographical possibility!

In recent times Upton Pyne, a village about four miles from Exeter in Devon, has been a favourite candidate for Barton. This hypothesis has given very much pleasure to Jane Austen devotees, and raised useful funds for the local Parish Church. Linda Findlay and a band of tireless volunteers have organised a delightful event called 'Jane Austen Day'. In fine midsummer weather attendees have been able to take a circular walk, visiting a local farmhouse at Woodrow Barton en route. A lively imagination with a disposition to be pleased might relate it to Barton Cottage. Delights such as a demonstration of riding modern side-saddle, open air dining, displays of ancient documents and entertaining talks have been enjoyed to the full. Who could resist Lily Neal's tempting bookstall from her Topsham Bookshop or the purchase of a little sachet of Upton Pyne lavender?

For those who retain a loyalty to The Book of Common Prayer hearing Regency Evensong conducted by Rev. Douglas Dettmer with a talented band playing Heritage Instruments such as The Serpent was a rare treat. The General Thanksgiving seems most aptly included in a service which while being evocative of the past can also be powerful in the present.

But whatever anyone's opinion of the location of Barton it is certainly a pleasure to admire some beautiful Devon countryside while bearing in mind Jane Austen's descriptions of the fictitious village Barton. She takes the opportunity to discuss the picturesque and mock the fanciful. The following words belong to William Gilpin, but I am sure that they would have found approval from Marianne Dashwood:

'The blasted tree has often a fine effect both in natural and in artificial landscape. In some scenes it is almost essential. When the dreary heath is spread before the eye and ideas if wildness and desolation are required, what more suitable accompaniment can be imaged than the blasted oak, ragged, scathed and leafless; shooting its peeled white branches thwart the gathering blackness of some rising storm….'.

Edward is ready with some common sense:

I like a fine prospect, but not on picturesque principles. I do not like crooked, twisted, blasted trees. I admire them much more if they are tall, straight and flourishing. I do not like ruined, tattered cottages. I am not fond of nettles, or thistles, or heath blossoms. I have more pleasure in a snug farm-house than a watch-tower — and a troop of tidy, happy villagers please me better than the finest banditti in the world."

Sense and Sensibility Chapter 18

The history of Upton Pyne certainly chimes with Jane's letter to her niece, Anna Austen LeFroy. Jane Austen is advising on Anna's literary efforts and recommends; *Three of four families in a country village is the very thing to work on.* Certainly in the Parish Church of Our Lady the names Larder, Pyne, Stafford and Northcote(family name of the Earls and Countesses of Iddesleigh) predominate. There is also mention of the generosity of Nicholas Williams who gained his wealth in trade from the 'black pit' of manganese in the vicinity.

In fact, all the ingredients that Jane Austen loved best are present in Upton Pyne. The Church would have satisfied her love of history, with its ancient medieval cross in the churchyard and the impressive west tower with statues of the Evangelists at the corners. The figure of King David may be seen on the South wall and over the west door is a carving of a benevolent Christ, blessing those who enter the church.

Even in such a seemingly retired spot the wider world has not been far away. Reverend John Walker was rector in Upton Pyne from 1720 to 1747. He was author of *The Sufferings of the Clergy* (during the Great Rebellion, 1642 to 1660). He is buried in the organ aisle. John Walker had previously been canon of Exeter Cathedral. *The Sufferings of the Clergy* is regarded by church historians as a valuable work of reference. It deals with the misfortunes of the Church of England clergy during and after the Civil War.

Another rector of this living was the uncle of John Gay. John Gay was the composer of The Beggar's Opera which is still enjoyed by audiences today and regularly performed. A fine monument to Rev. James Gay is on the wall and poignantly his little son, also James, who died in 1702 at the age of five years, has his tombstone under the altar.

In a village there must be a Great House. The Pynes relates to Jane Austen's description in being hidden out of sight of Woodrow Barton by a hill. In *Sense and Sensibility* Mrs. Dashwood and her daughters, Elinor, Marianne and Margaret are dispossessed by the legal claim of the son and heir of Mr. Dashwood's first wife. They take refuge in Barton Cottage on the estate of a cousin in Devonshire. This cousin is the wealthy Sir John Middleton who lives in the *large and handsome house* known as Barton, in Barton Park. The name Barton is frequently used in Devon. At Upton Pyne the elegant Queen Anne manor house, 'Pynes' was designed by Inigo Jones. It was formerly the home of the Northcote family. The House has recently undergone extensive restoration

At the gateway to the drive are stone pineapples. These were a symbol of hospitality in the eighteenth century, as they cost a fortune to produce in heated houses with the expensive glass construction only affordable by the very rich. The government tax on glass was the inspiration for the saying 'daylight robbery'. This is still applied when cost price of anything exceeds what ought to be charged; very apt in the case of light or air!

In Pride and Prejudice Elizabeth pays a formal call at Pemberley as politeness requires. It is a somewhat awkward occasion as she is not a favourite with some of the house party, notably Miss Bingley who has not yet despaired of marrying Mr Darcy and knows he admires Elizabeth. The atmosphere eases with the appearance of refreshments. As Jane Austen remarks: *though they could not all talk, they could eat; and the beautiful pyramids of grapes, nectarines and peaches soon collected them round the table.* These hot-house delicacies were irresistible!

It is said that people would borrow them for table centre decorations and return them uneaten after the party to be passed on to someone else!

Might Jane Austen have heard of another place *within 4 miles northward of Exeter*?

It is an interesting thought that Jane Austen had almost certainly heard this phrase in conversation. It has just the sort of ring that might make an aspiring author prick up her ears. It could have well described the location of a place whose existence was known to Jane Austen through the family friend and Reverend Austen's former pupil, Richard Buller.   I am indebted to Deidre Le Faye's scholarship for the following observation as for so many other erudite notes on Jane Austen's letters.

This is the village of Stoke Cannon. Richard Buller was one of the sons of the Bishop of Exeter. According to a custom of the time Richard was responsible for three different parishes or 'livings'. As well as being vicar of Colyton, where he lived and rector of West Buckland he was also perpetual curate of Stoke Canon. This could well have been described to Jane Austen as having the same proximity and direction.

All things considered, the setting of Upton Pyne makes this village an attractive place to visit in its own right. It fits the cheerful description of Barton as a *pleasant, fertile spot, well wooded and rich in pasture.* This tone in the novel contrasts with the sadness of Elinor and Marianne at their shocking dispossession which begins the story. It is a hopeful sign for the future:

High hills rose immediately behind, and at no great distance on each side; some of which were open downs, the others cultivated and woody. ..The prospect in front was more extensive; it commanded the whole of the valley, and reached into the country beyond. The hills which surrounded the cottage terminated the valley in that direction; under another name, and in another course, it branched out again between two of the steepest of them.

The open vista, full of promise also calls up the description of Adam and Eve leaving the Garden of Eden in John Milton's *Paradise Lost* (in this case the wonderful Norland Park):

The world was all before them, where to choose

Their place of rest, and Providence their guide

A rather more allegorical interpretation may be inferred later. We are told that the valley which branches away from the main situation of the cottage is narrow, winding and leads to an ancient respectable looking mansion at Allenham. As events turn out the passionate Marianne is indeed led up a narrow and winding path by a respectable-<u>looking</u> gentleman. Shakespeare, with whose works Jane Austen was most throroughly acquainted, might have described it as *the primrose path of dalliance*. Willoughby turns out to be a seducer. When his behaviour results in his disinheritance he switches his affections away from Marianne in order to marry for money. But after that hint of unhappiness to come, we are swept away from the dirt of the valleys below to the high downs with Marianne and Margaret enjoying the high winds.

Clever Miss Jane Austen-how she repays careful reading to fathom the layers of meaning in her brilliant work.

Chapter Six - Drama and Romance

Jane Austen and Romance

How could an unmarried lady of the Eighteenth Century, constrained by the customs of society, write such brilliant comedies of manners, love and marriage with such insight? We wonder at her capacity to describe relationships and wonder how her personal experiences of romance might have influenced her writing.

The tradition goes that thwarted in her affection for Tom LeFroy, Jane created her own fictional hero in Mr. Fitzwilliam Darcy. This hero was 'wish fulfilment', the gist of their romance might be resolved by an imagined exchange:

Elizabeth: "I've embarrassing relations"

Darcy: "Never mind, mi 'dear, I'm taking you to Derbyshire. Your whole family will be welcome at Christmas; your father may take refuge under my roof at any time; though you will understand I cannot receive Wickham"

Elizabeth: "I've no money"

Darcy: "No matter, I've more than enough for two!"

Jane Austen's Suitors

But what can we surmise from letters, hints and family tradition?

New Year, 1796.

Thomas Langlois LeFroy had come to Hampshire to visit relations.

It was not a long visit and we only have the details from Jane's letters to Cassandra with their light bantering tone. But it does seem to have been a mutual attraction, first love. Unfortunately Jane had numerous brothers to be launched into the world and a dowry was not much of a possibility. Without a fortune she might expect an offer from a respectable clergyman. The requirements are heartlessly listed by Lady Catherine de Bourgh in *Pride and Prejudice;* gentility, some accomplishments and conversation and a boundless ability to make a small stipend stretch to cover household expenses.

For all too short a time Jane and Tom danced, talked and even flirted. His watchful Aunt and hostess, Anne LeFroy, who was a mentor to Jane, was probably responsible for whisking Tom away to try and avoid heartbreak for her young friend. An improvident father meant that he had womenfolk depending on him. His Great Uncle, who was paying for his legal training, must be appeased. Tradition has it that at the end of his life he remembered her with affection

'It was a boy's love'.

1797-8

It is guesswork to say that to make amends Mrs Le Froy presented an alternative beau for Jane's consideration. This was Rev. Samuel Blackall. (1770-1842) He was a Fellow of Emmanuel College, but maybe even at this point he had made a private plan not to marry until he had secured the ecclesiastical living at North (Great) Cadbury in Somerset. When this eventually happened in 1812 the new Rector briskly courted and married Susannah Lewis, daughter of James Lewis of Clifton, Bristol (formerly of Jamaica) in January 1813. It all sounds very sensible. Jane comments in a letter to Francis - Saturday 3rd –Tuesday 6th July, 1813

that this was *the very living which we remembered his talking and wishing for.*

Following his introduction to the Austen family he had prudently written to Mrs LeFroy:

I am very sorry to hear of Mrs. Austen's illness. It would give me particular pleasure to have an opportunity of improving my acquaintance with that family-with a hope of creating to myself a nearer interest, but at present I cannot indulge any expectation of it

Jane Austen is somewhat justifiably scornful of this irritatingly bumptious and arrogant self-regard:

Less love and more sense in it than sometimes appeared before.

He has obviously been tempted, but prudently withdrawn. Like Rev. Elton in *Emma* wordly considerations will govern his choice of a bride.

Jane Austen rightly predicts:

It will all go on exceedingly well, and decline away in a very reasonable manner.

Her reaction to his marriage is a throwaway remark, and a rather spiteful dig:

He was a peice of Perfection, noisy Perfection himself which I always recollect with regard.

I would wish Miss Lewis to be of a silent turn & rather ignorant, but naturally intelligent and eager to learn;-fond of cold veal pies, green tea in the afternoon & a green window blind at night.

He has passed up bright vivacity and deserves a colourless existence!

1799

The presence of the Cheshire Militia brought an unnamed admirer to the local balls and assemblies.

But the nameless and dateless lover who most intrigues us, the one who may well have meant more than all the rest, remains tantalisingly unknown. He is spoken of freely among family members. We have to be content with fragments as small as some ancient parchment which has been burnt and scattered by time. Piecing it together to make some sense constantly tempts us to complete it with fancy and guesswork, for we have few primary sources for rigorous scholarship.

According to tradition this young man was a clergyman, the brother of a Doctor in a seaside resort visited by Jane Austen and her family on one of their summer excursions from Bath to Devon and Dorset.

The fullest account of this love affair comes from Jane's sister Cassandra, and possibly Jane herself, via her first niece, Anna who was particularly close to her aunts. She writes:

The Austens with their two daughters were once at Teignmouth, the date of that visit was not later than 1802, but besides this they were once travelling in Devonshire, moving about from place to

place, and I think that tour was before they left Steventon in 1801, perhaps as early as 1798 or 1799. It was while they were so travelling, according to Aunt Cassandra's account many years afterwards, that they somehow made acquaintance with a gentleman .... He and Aunt Jane mutually attracted each other, and such was his charm that even Aunt Cassandra thought him worthy of her sister. They parted on the understanding that he was to come to 'Steventon, but instead came I know not how long after a letter from his brother to say that he was dead.

There is no record of Jane's affliction, but I think this attachment must have been very deep. Aunt Cassandra had so warm a regard for him that some years after her sister's death, she took a great deal of trouble to find out and see again his brother.

Cassandra's attitude is the vital factor which makes this ring true. Such a protective sister would not have given any sign of approval, nor spoken of such a personal matter to anyone, without good reason.

We are left with the pithy observation of Jane Austen's great-nephew, Lord Brabourne that the fellow *very provokingly died suddenly*

It was by no means a rare thing for people of that time to die quickly for want of modern medicines. There is a rumour that this gentleman was poisoned by water from a well in Sidmouth, which is perfectly possible. There is a theory that he is actually Rev. Samuel Blackall, whose brother was a doctor in Totnes. The proposal goes that he returned to toy with Miss Jane Austen's affections and broke her hear

Constance Pilgrim, in her book *'Dear Jane'* makes a delightful and compelling case for the nameless and dateless lover being Captain John Wordsworth, the younger brother of the poet William Wordsworth.

In February 1805, John Wordsworth, Commander of the East Indiaman The Earl of Abergavenny, set off from Portsmouth towards Weymouth . He had misgivings with good reason. If you visit Portland Bill you will be told of the necessity of the lighthouse there because of the counter currents offshore, which are treacherous. John wrote:

The Commodore intends to go through The Needles, a passage I do not like much, but I hope will be attended with no accident

It was his third voyage in command and sadly his last. The westerly gale off Portland Bill on 5th February 1805, battered and waterlogged the vessel, while the well-known strong currents off the point forced the ship on and off the rocks. Frantically pumping and baling, the crew could not save her and she sank. The entire cargo was lost, and over half the people on board, including the captain, John Wordsworth, whose body was recovered after 6 weeks.

Mrs. Pilgrim weaves a delightful story. It is heart-stopping romantic, and has echoes from Jane Austen's novels showing how Jane might have transposed real life incidents to her writing.

There is the imagined scenario of an early introduction in The Assembly Rooms at Bath, where as an experienced East India Man John might have impressed Jane with his knowledge of muslins (he sent a gown of Indian muslin to his sister-in-law, Mary Hutchinson who married William Wordsworth, which she liked very much). This is just like the hero of *Northanger Abbey*, who impresses Mrs. Allen, whose passion is for fashion, with his knowledge. Jane demonstrates that it is perfectly gentlemanly to know about trade,

though some would scorn Wordsworth for being in what might be called 'The Merchant Navy', rather than what Mary Crawford calls 'The King's Service'(Royal Navy) in Mansfield Park.

By investigation worthy of Miss Marple, Mrs. Pilgrim shows how John Wordsworth moved in the same circles as Jane and might have been present at Lyme, as she refers to Lyme Regis.

John Wordsworth could have been an early suitor and rejected for the same reasons as Anne Eliot rejects Frederick Wentworth in *Persuasion*; the long and uncertain climb to prosperity he had before him, coupled with Jane's lack of a fortune. Disapproval of his being an employee of the East India Company and lack of financial security might prompt intervention by concerned friends, such as Mrs. Leroy.

After this estrangement there is a suggestion that they correspond on the subject of William's poems, but encounter another setback when Jane is sent a copy of York Herald announcing Mr. Wordsworth's marriage, but not making it clear which brother it is.

Just such a tangle is used to dramatic effect in Sense and Sensibility when Elinor mistakenly believes Edward Ferrars to have married, when in fact it is Robert Ferrars the older brother, with the money, who has been preferred by Miss Lucy Steele.

There are imagined chance meetings in London and Bath, a secret engagement, snatches of happy meetings in Kent and on The Isle of Wight. It may not have a word of truth, but it is a good read.

What we do know is that in December 1802 Jane famously accepted a sensible proposal from Harris Bigg-Wither. Harris was six years younger than Jane Austen. Three of his sisters, Elizabeth, Catherine and Alethea Bigg (only the boys took the additional family name of Wither) were great friends with Cassandra and Jane Austen. Harris was the heir to Manydown Park He could offer Jane security. She would be chatelaine of a large country house. It was a full time occupation, with the distinct possibility of a baby every year.

Once her acceptance had been given and the excitement died down, Jane may have had time for serious thought. She was already the author of three books, as yet unpublished. Her family circle was her whole security. They supported and understood what she was trying to do. But if Jane Austen were a married woman, writing and the dream of publication would have to be laid aside. She may well have decided that her feelings were just not strong enough to sacrifice her creativity.

Jane explained as gently as she could then she and Cassandra got James to assist them home. Harris married very happily, had ten children and lived the life of a country squire.

Jane Austen was without doubt an attractive and lively member of her circle. In 1805 the clergyman Brook-Edward Bridges courted her. He was younger brother to her sister-in-law, Elizabeth. It is thought that she discouraged him because of the proximity of their relationship through her brother Edward.

Jane Austen was a sensitive person. In those days it might be described as having great delicacy of feeling. The fact was that her brother Edward had inherited great wealth as the heir to his adopted parents. The Knight family were cousins of the Austen family and were their benefactors. Brook-Edward Bridges was also well to do.

Jane Austen could reasonably feel a poor relation. She might well be concerned that a marriage might produce ill-natured criticism that she had somehow presumed upon her connection and taken advantage of the family connection to marry for money.

Exmouth Theatre and Mrs. Piozzi

Jane Austen certainly knew of and enjoyed the work of Mrs Piozzi and had adopted her writing style in fun while composing a letter to Cassandra. Mrs Piozzi was previously known as Mrs Hester Thrale. She survived her much older husband in what was a difficult marriage.

Dr Johnson was a valued family friend and the three were a mutually helpful support to each other through good times and bad. Hester Thrale was hostess to his Literary Club of intellectuals.

After her husband's death Hester fell deeply in love with an Italian musician, Gabriel Piozzi. She employed him as a singing teacher. But when she told Dr Johnson that she intended to remarry he lost his temper.

Of course Dr Johnson regretted this, but she would not meet him again. The marriage to Gabriel Piozzi was an exceedingly happy one.

Because of the high quality of theatre available in Bath, Jane Austen may not have attended many productions while at the seaside resorts. But there was theatre, albeit of an itinerant kind, and these operations were supposed not to be very profitable.

We have the odd glimpse of theatrical treats, Certainly Mrs. Piozzi wrote extensively. She was a resident in Gay Street, Bath. In 1788 she penned this rather lovely prologue for the Exmouth Theatre .

'By many a wave, by many a tempest tost

Our shipwrecked hopes are cast on Devon's coast

Where the soft season swells the ripening grain,

And verdure brightens with refreshing rain,

Where lightenings seldom glare, or thunder roar

And chilling blasts forget their freezing power'

Chapter Seven – A Jane Austen Treasure in Torquay

<u>Jane Austen's Letter to Cassandra, January 1799.</u>

This long, newsy, letter, written by Jane to her sister to wish her a very happy birthday is kept on the English Riviera, at Torquay. At the time of Jane Austen Tor Bay played its own important part in the wars with France. On the 7th August 1815 , in the waters off the Devon coast, Napoleon was transferred from the *Bellerophon* to *Northumberland* for the voyage to St. Helena and his final imprisonment

The letter was presented to the Torquay Natural History Society by Hester Forbes-Julian nee Pengelly. She was the daughter of William Pengelly, a notable Victorian. By profession a teacher, this son of a Cornish sea captain was famed locally as archaeologist, botanist, geologist, natural historian and philanthropist. The local Pengelly Caves Studies Trust bear his name and he was the moving spirit in the creation of the Torquay Museum..

Hester inherited her Worcestershire Grandmother's collection of documents and added to them. She was an enthusiastic autograph hunter. Perhaps her collection was admired at her legendary tea parties.

This letter was one selected by Cassandra to be given to Fanny, Lady Knatchbull. Cassandra took immense pains to distribute letters to members of the family for whom they might hold special interest. Fanny would have doubtless been amused by the anecdote about her second son, George. Though inherited by Lord Brabourne, it is believed that Hester purchased the letter in a sale in June 1893.

The letter begins: Tuesday 8 –Wednesday 9 January 1 *Steventon*

My Dear Cassandra

*You must read your letters over **five** times in future before you send*

them then perhaps you may find them as entertaining as I do.- I laughed at several parts of the one which I am now answering.

The original letter has a trace of a red wafer seal and the postmark OVERTON. The hand is clear, precise and legible

'an artist cannot do anything slovenly' Jane wrote on another occasion. [Letter 17-18 November 1798].

The letter of 1799 has begun with compliments on Cassandra's letter writing skills which have amused her sister. Jane's admiration for her elder sibling is well known and survived into their adulthood. As it progresses we feel we are in the room. *'I have now attained the true art of letter writing which we are told is to express on paper exactly what we would say to the same person by word of mouth'* [letter-3rd-5th January 1801]

At the time of the letter Cassandra is staying with their brother Edward, his wife Elizabeth and their five children at Godmersham Park in Kent.

It is always slightly uncomfortable to stay with wealthy relations. Elizabeth's reported remarks about Jane copying out music are included. They have flicked Jane on the raw and she responds with wit and spirit. The comfortable circumstances in which Edward and Elizabeth are placed seems to strike a false note with Jane and challenges her sense of fairness.

But what would Jane Austen be without that refreshing candour which prompts the comment:

'I am tolerably glad to hear that Edward's income is so good a one- as glad as I can be at anybody's being rich besides You & me' The behaviour of Edward's adopted mother, Mrs. Knight, in giving up Godmersham is remarked upon as being laced with an hefty measure of self-interest. The sweetener for handing over the onerous role of Chatelaine of such a large estate is an annuity of £2,000; financial benefit without responsibility.

Jane Austen's eyesight is known to have been poor and her cold seems to be making it worse. She didn't like to admit she might have to let Mrs Austen write for her. Luckily her eyes get better.

Ready for the Ball

The Kempshott Ball is mentioned with happy anticipation. Charles is expected and Jane has made sure he is invited, though she has not organised anyone for him to partner; just as well as it turns out.

It is sometimes claimed that Jane Austen does not mention the momentous events that were rocking the world she inhabited. But the mere description of Jane's proposed ensemble for the Ball faithfully reflects the spirit of this moment in history.

Jane's outfit demonstrates the excitement generated by Nelson's victory at the Battle of the Nile, about six months before this letter was written. The deep green waters of the Nile became green shoes. They often had ribbons of crocodile yellow. Jane is to lay aside her white ' sattin' cap in favour of a fez-shaped Marmalouc (marmaluke) cap. Such caps and turbans often sported an egret's plume – the Nelson rose feather. Such an item is treasured by her descendants still.

Her essential accessory for the heat of the ballroom has had a narrow escape – the white fan, which was nearly thrown in the river by George.

'Sweet little George' refers to George –Thomas, third child of Jane's brother Edward, who had just turned four years old. His babyish lisp had caused him to christen himself 'Itty Dordy'. His mischievous scampering along the river bank with Aunt Jane's fan was no doubt regarded with mock horror by the adults. An affectionate and somewhat indulgent attitude of the Georgians to their children is portrayed or maybe it is just George with his *inventive Genius as to face-making'* was rather cute.

Jane Austen treats Cassandra to a good account of the evening. Students of eighteenth century etiquette will be amused by her enjoying *'sitting down two Dances in preference to having Lord Bolton's eldest son for my Partner, who danced too ill to be endured'!* Polite manners would have prevented her from accepting an invitation from anyone else.. Charles could not get away in time to be there. We all know the insecurity which leads to the remark

'I do not think I was much in request'. She wisely concludes

'One's consequence you know varies so much at times without any particular reason'

The letter has one last treat to yield in the first mention of a certain work of fiction known at that time as *First Impressions'* , the darling child that grew up to become *Pride and Prejudice.*

The Benefactress who donated the letter to the Museum, Hester, married Henry Forbes-Julian, a professional metallurgist and indefatigable traveller; a Buchanesque figure in the mould of Richard Hannay. He was due to leave England on a journey in spring 1911 and Hester was to accompany him. She was too ill to travel. To hasten his plans, Henry Forbes Julian was transferred on to the *Ttanic* He perished, but Hester is classed as a survivor.

Torquay Museum was originally founded in 1844. There is a pleasant and lively feeling of welcome. It is at the heart of local cultural life with many exhibitions of topical and local interest. Yet at the time of writing the future of the Torquay Museum is in jeopardy. The proposed necessary cuts in funding are so savage that it may not survive. All I can do is ask you to join me in doing whatever you can to raise awareness of its worth as the home of treasures and a vital community resource.

Chapter Eight – Plots and Recognition

A Brief Introduction to Jane Austen's Novels for the Curious.

Jane Austen is known mainly for six completed novels. Their plots centre upon love and marriage. But the genius of their authoress means that they are witty and shrewd portraits of society as lived by the Gentry class in eighteenth century England. The characters and humour in the novels have a universal appeal which has earned Jane Austen lasting fame. It is really important to remember that her characters are not pale imitations of people she knew. Jane Austen is reported as having spoken to her friend Mrs Ann Barratt of Alton on this matter.

Jane Austen expressed a very great dread of what she called an *'invasion of social proprieties'* She said she thought it fair to note peculiarities, weaknesses and even special phrases but it was her desire to create not to reproduce and at the same time said *'I am too proud of my own gentlemen ever to admit they were merely Mr A or Mr B'*

Miss Jane Austen also wrote various works when in her teenage years, which are referred to as The Juvenilia , and two uncompleted novels.

Before her move from Steventon, Jane Austen had written three novels in their first forms.

Northanger Abbey (published 1818) concerns the teenager Catherine Morland, an enthusiastic reader of gothic novels, filled with every sort of murder and mayhem. She is prone to confuse fact with fantasy, but ensnares Henry Tilney by the simple strategy of adoring him.

Sense and Sensibility (1811) concerns two sisters, the sensible Elinor and the headstrong Marianne. Poverty and Disinheritance forces them to Devon where after many hard life lessons they are rewarded with husbands

Pride and Prejudice (1813)reminds us to be wary of First Impressions as the five Bennet sisters negotiate society.

Later she revised these works substantially and three more completed novels joined them.

Emma (1816) in the story of that name, has wealth, position and happiness and cannot resist matchmaking amongst her circle, with terrible results. It conforms to Jane Austen's preferred formula of three or four families in a country village. The action revolves round the estate at Donwell Abbey, Emma's home at Hartfield, the home of Mr and Mrs Weston and the households of Farmer Martin, Mrs and Miss Bates and of course, The Rectory. The story is set against the background of the English country year. Although it is far inland, Weymouth features and at the conclusion Emma attains her wish to see the sea as it is her honeymoon destination.

Mansfield Park (1814) is a story of virtue with a strong moral tone. It follows the fortunes of Fanny Price. At the beginning of the story she is only 10 years old and sent from her chaotic home in Portsmouth to live with her Aunt and Uncle Bertram at Mansfield Park. Her firmness of character and quiet determination ensure that she becomes the guardian of the house and mainstay of the family.

Persuasion (1818) is a masterpiece with an older heroine, who gets a well-deserved second chance of happiness. Although in love with him in her teens, Ann sent Captain Wentworth away upon the advice of a family friend , as he was yet to succeed in his naval career and they were both young. Can she retrieve the situation now he has come back into her life by chance? He is a successful millionaire, minded to find a wife, but still offended by her rejection ten years before.

Miss Austen also began a novel entitled *The Watsons*, but laid it aside after 17,000 words.

Ill health forced her to lay down her pen before she could finish her final work, *Sanditon*. This promising novel traces the rise of a seaside resort under the enthusiastic efforts of Mr William Parker.

Nowadays we can enjoy the filmed versions of the books, as well as many other prequels, sequels and spin-offs from the original novels.

Magazines, Tweets, blogs songs, plays and Festivals celebrate Jane Austen's work throughout the World. She would be amazed, but I hope gratified by our interest.

A Successful Author

We have two possible images of Jane Austen from this time in her life. In the National Portrait Gallery in London there is one of the only authenticated portraits of Jane Austen, which her sister, Cassandra began but did not finish. It is a miniature in water colour and ink. Only the face is completed. Jane is shown in her mid-thirties. She is seated with her arms folded. She looks somewhat uneasy. For those who love her work it is a pleasing glimpse of someone who does not dissemble. It is defiant. It seems to have

been begun in an odd moment at home, perhaps after hard morning writing. I wish I could see whether Jane Austen's fingers were inky. There is a completely contrasting image, which is not authenticated. But it makes me tingle. It shows a confident woman, secure in her powers, presenting a brave face to the world.

Jane Austen after a sketch by Stanier-Clarke

In November 1815 Jane visits Carlton House, residence of The Prince Regent. Her guide is Rev. James Stanier Clarke, the Prince's domestic chaplain and librarian at the Charlton House. His commission is to invite Jane Austen to dedicate her novel *Emma* to his Royal Highness the Prince of Wales. Jane Austen may well have disapproved of the well-known excesses of the Prince Regent. But *Prinny* was a patron of the Arts. He kept sets of her work at all his residences. Jane Austen was gracious and the result was a gracefully worded tribute at the beginning of the novel.

Rev. James Stanier Clarke was an enthusiastic amateur artist, whose fascination with the literary world led him to record the likeness of such authors as George Eliot, which have been praised for their accuracy. It seems he might well have been inspired to make a swift sketch of Miss Jane Austen.

He thought highly enough of the result to cut it out and incorporate it into a picture he executed. This shows a woman in her thirties, wearing a stylish outfit.

If it is Jane Austen, and I do so hope it might be, she is wearing a simple white gown of the period, but over it is a fashionable garment of the time, part cape, and part shawl with extravagant ruffles. Jane Austen describes having a similar garment in one of her early surviving letters to Cassandra. On her head is a delightful hat with feathers. Her hands are tucked inside an enormous hand-warmer, known then as a muff, made of fur. It speaks of someone who loves fashion and going up to Town. Her dear brother Henry has been ill, but is out of danger. He has received the best of attention, care and books to read in his convalescence from Charles Thomas Haden FRCS. Jane Austen describes him as *something between a Man and an Angel*

Letter to Cassandra 2nd December 1815

Mr Haden was charming and urbane. He seems to have enjoyed the company at Hans Place and it appears that Jane was gratified by some intelligent conversation and support at such a difficult time. It was possibly a little intoxicating, causing her to bloom and be cheerful.

She is about to have her fourth novel published by the most fashionable publisher of the day, Mr John Murray.

Chapter Nine - Hampshire -1809-1817

Domestic life in rural leisure passed

Oh, friendly to the best pursuits

Friendly to thought, to virtue, and to peace,

Domestic life in rural leisure pass'd

William Cowper

Thanks to the generosity of Edward Austen Knight , Jane Austen's final eight years were spent with her Mother, family friend Martha Lloyd and Sister Cassandra in the village of Chawton in Hampshire, close to her brother's Chawton House and Estate. *...placed in the midst of those who loved her' Emma ch 55*

It was just the secure environment in which her genius could thrive. She drew constantly upon her experiences and knowledge of The West Country for her work. Jane Austen's creative power was undiminished right to the end of her life.

Sanditon, the novel Jane Austen did not have time to complete, tells the story of an entrepreneur, Mr William Parker. He wishes to develop a seaside resort on the South Coast. Jane Austen visited Worthing for a very successful holiday after leaving Bath. She also had experience of other coastal locations. The nature of her skill is that we can never be sure which elements were inspired by which place, as they are blended into their own unique and different creation. But it is true to say that Mr. Richard Hollis, the developer of Lyme Regis might well be in her mind as she wrote.

Jane Austen allowed her imagination to roam through this imagined watering place. Sacrificed to her husband's ambitions, the long suffering Mrs Parker lives in a bracing position, exposed to healthy sea breezes and thinks longingly of her snug inland dwelling with its orchards.

Mr Parker has a firm grasp on the essentials which his resort must provide to be a popular success. He knows that the benefits of his seaside location must be exploited. Invalids are drawn to anywhere that might provide a cure. In an age of few proven medical remedies anything that bolstered health was seized upon with enthusiasm.

In Sanditon Mr Parker yearns to attract a doctor to attend them:

'convinced that the advantage of a <u>medical man</u> at hand would very materially promote the rise and prosperity of the place, would in fact tend to bring a prodigious influx…his own sisters, who were sad invalids…could hardly be expected to hazard themselves in a place where they could not have immediate medical advice'

Comedy is supplied by the arrival of Mr Parker's sisters and their strapping brother Arthur, who is a true hypochondriac, imagining everything to be wrong with him, while still able to enjoy food and wine in large quantities. At a tea party the lovely Charlotte Heywood is amazed to see his 'weak cocoa' coming forth:

..In a very fine, dark coloured stream-and at the same moment, his Sisters both crying out 'OH! Arthur, you get your Cocoa stronger and stronger every evening

His sisters also protest about the amount of butter he is spreading on his toast:

Charlotte could hardly contain herself as she saw him watching his sisters, while he scrupulously scraped off almost as much butter as he put on, and then seize the odd moment for adding a great dab just before it went into his mouth

Jane Austen's heart must have been very heavy indeed as she laid aside her pen in March 1817, unable to go on fighting the illness which had taken her strength. She was to travel to Winchester, so that she could be under the care of Mr Lyford and the surgeons at the hospital.

Her will is dated 27th April. Everything is for her dear sister Cassandra, apart from a legacy of £50 for Henry who continued to struggle financially after the failure of his banking enterprise. There is also the loving touch of £50 for Madame Bigeon, his housekeeper, who lost her life savings in the collapse of the bank.

One month to the day later a frail young woman is helped into her brother's carriage. Her spiky sister-in-law has given her generous permission for this loan, as it doesn't inconvenience her personally and the gesture looks good to the family.

An anxious sister tucks shawls and rugs about her as if enough blankets would protect her from the jolts of the road. Her devoted brother Henry making light of the rain which has begun, mounts his horse and checks that his young nephew William has tightened his horse's girth and has his stirrups level and long enough.

Mrs Austen hovers at the door, aware that the younger generation are supporting each other in the way she has trained them to do. She is a helpless bystander, absorbing the blow and hiding the hurt of the occasion beneath a long practised appearance of resignation. Her tears for her brave, bright incomprehensible daughter will be private ones.

The Hampshire countryside has the fresh green of early summer about it. The trees drip an incessant tattoo on the roof of the carriage. Jane can almost feel the wetness trickle down past the collars of the coats and steadily drench the faithful escorts. The hedgerow is full of frothy Queen Anne's Lace and Cow Parsley, lining the route like countless country lasses, wearing white for Whitsuntide .

Jane finds it utterly exhausting, watching the uncooperative weather and worrying about her menfolk. It would have been

so much more bearable on a fine day.

Jane Austen put up a gallant fight, but nothing could be done, other than to make her as comfortable as possible. She died with Cassandra supporting her head on a pillow on 18th July at 4.30 a.m.

She was forty one years old.

> It is not growing like a tree
> In bulk doth make Man better be;
> Or standing long an oak, three hundred year,
> To fall a log at last, dry, bald, and sere:
> A lily of a day
> Is fairer far in May,
> Although it fall and die that night—
> It was the plant and flower of light.
> In small proportions we just beauties see;
> And in short measures life may perfect be.

Ben Jonson 1572-1637

Bibliography

This is a short selection of the many books and articles consulted]

Austen, Caroline-Mary-Craven-My Aunt Jane –JASociety 1991

Austen,Jane & Family Family- Poems-Ed David Selwyn –JASociety 1996

Austen,Jane-Letters Ed. Deidre Le Faye 3rd Edition 1995

Austen,Jane – Novels – Ed. R.W.Chapman O.U.P. 1965-67

Austen,Jane – Poems & Favourite Poems –Ed. Douglas Brooks Davies .J.M.Dent 1998

Austen, Jane-The History of Mr Harley and othet Juvenilia

Austen, Jane-Wit and Wisdom

Austen-Leigh,Richard-Austen Papers 1704-1856 –London 1942

Black, Jeremy –Georgian Devon –Mint Press 2003

 Bath Royal Literary and Scientific Institution. "The Combe Hay Caisson Lock" Retrieved 2006

Burney, Frances – *Journals and Letters* selected and with introduction by Peter Sabor and Lars E. Troide – Penguin 2001

Byrne, Paula-Jane Austen and The Theatre

Coard, David – Vanishing Bath Vols 1-3

Collins, Irene – Jane Austen and The Clergy

Fowles, John –A short History of Lyme Regis –Dovecote Press 1991

Freeman, Jean- Jane Austen in Bath –JASociety Revised 2002

Gadd, David –Georgian Summer-Adams & Dart 1971

Griffiths, G.D- History of Teignmouth 1965

Ham, Elizabeth-The Diary of Elizabeth Ham

I've been a silly, I'll admit ; I really am not proud of it.

Jane Austen would with great distaste have viewed the errors of my haste.

Here is a list for you to use; though this is but a poor excuse.

I am just grateful for my friends who helped me here to make amends.

Please do not let it spoil your fun in reading – Thank you everyone!

Stepping Westward - Errata –p.9 semi-colon missing before quote-p.11Sri Lanka-p.15 Fulwar –p.28 Mr not Dr Perry-p.31 Mrs Wallis not Fitzpatrick-p.43 James became Rector after Mr Austen's death-p.44 Austen family not Austens'-p.52 with what happy feelings of escape-p.59 & 74 Frances-p.65 Guillotine-p.74 Newfoundland not Northumberland-p.78 Elinor-p.82 & 124 Anne Elliot; Harville would have been Benwick's brother in law after his sister Fanny's marriage, but she died before the wedding-p.87 efforts-p.88 Mrs Shervington is a collateral descendant; Weymouth-p.101Jennings's-p.102 William Elliot;Seaton in Devon-p.104,109,114 Lefroy with small f-106 &134 Deirdre(2 r's); for 'them' read pineapples-p.107 Canon is the correct spelling-p.113 heart-p.118 second brother, not son-p.121 1912-p.124 Vicarage not Rectory;

P.61 the seine is the net; seining is the method.

Hargood-Ash, J- History of the Parish of Weston, Bath

Haynes, C.- The Most Rebellious Town in Devon: The Monmouth Rebellion of 1685 and the citizens of Colyton - 2003

Honan, Park –Jane Austen: her life-Orion 1997

Keats, John – Letters

Lane, Maggie-Jane Austen and Lyme Regis – JASociety 2003

Le Faye, Deidre- Jane Austen and Her Regency World

Meller, H. –A La Ronde -National Trust Guide 1993

National Trust Guide– Saltram

Nicholson, D. Was Jane Austen Happy in Bath?

Norman, Dr Andrew - Unrequited Love – 2009-History Press

Phillips, M. Picture of Lyme Regis and Environs 1817 –facsimile Dorset County Museum

Pilgrim, Constance- Dear Jane

Plymouth Council – Joshua Reynolds

Poplawski, Paul-A Jane Austen Encyclopedia-Greenwood-USA-1998

Quin, Vera Jane Austen Visits London Cappella Archive 2008

Radcliffe, Mrs A- Mysteries of Udolpho

Rogers, Pat-The rise and fall of Gout –TLS 20th March 1981

Russell, P.M.G.-A Short History and Guide to the Church of Our Lady, Upton Pyne –Phillips Print Bureau 1978

Russell, P.- A history of Torquay and the famous anchorage of Torbay -Torquay Natural History Society-1960

Somersetshire Coal Canal (Society). "History of the Caisson Lock On the Somersetshire Coal Canal .

Southam, Brian – Jane Austen and The Navy- 2000

Snaddon, Brenda-The Last Promenade-Sydney Gardens, Bath Millstream Books 2000

The Exeter Flying Post 1775-1806-West Country Studies Centre

The History of the Oxford Militia

Townsend, An Officer of the Long Parliament

Uglow, Jenny – Dr Johnson, His Club and Other Friends-National Portrait Gallery 1998

Wallis, J.- Guide to Sidmouth, 1810

White, Rev Gilbert –Natural History and Antiquities of Selborne -1768

Wordsworth, William – Poems, 1807 'Stepping Westward'

Acknowledgements:

I have made every conscientious effort to obtain appropriate permissions to quote from published sources and for the use of images. If there is any difficulty I shall be most glad to know of it. I heartily thank those who have responded to my enquiries with such gracious responses.

So many people have offered support and encouragement to me in fulfilling my promise to Richard.

I gratefully acknowledge the wisdom and knowledge of Deidre Le Faye, without whom I would not have had the courage to proceed at all. In particular the notes to the Letters have helped me to be precise. The legacy of her scholarship has been an example and inspiration to me.

Maggie Lane, Hazel Jones and Stephen Mahoney are the most amazingly accomplished and knowledgeable experts and thanks to all my companions whose friendship at the Jane Austen Society South West Branch has helped me on many occasions.

All my valued colleagues at The Jane Austen Centre, especially The Proprietor David Baldock also, Judith Lacey and Sue Hughes , not forgetting Glenys without whom I'd not have had a thing to wear in the early days!

Tim Bullamore deserves thanks for being the long-suffering recipient of my hopeful articles for Jane Austen's Regency World Magazine.